Shore, Pier
and Boat
Fishing

Shore, Pier and Boat Fishing

Full of Top Tips on How To Catch More Sea Fish

JIM WHIPPY

Abbeydale Press

ISBN 978-1-86147-242-7

1 3 5 7 9 10 8 6 4 2

Published by Abbeydale Press
an imprint of Bookmart Ltd
Registered number 2372865
Trading as Bookmart Ltd
Blaby Road, Wigston, Leicester
LE18 4SE, England

Produced by Omnipress Limited, UK
Cover design by Omnipress Limited, UK

Printed in Dubai

THE AUTHOR

JIM WHIPPY has been a sea angler all his life having
been brought up on the coast of East Sussex. After
winning his local club boat championships several
times he progressed to win the European Cod
Championship, the Plymouth International, the YYS
International Challenge and the National Boat League
Final. His consistent form won him a place in the NFSA
England team competing in the World Boat
Championships on five occasions, winning team silver
and team bronze. Jim has edited three fishing
publications, *Sea Angling News*, *Total Sea Fishing*,
Boat Fishing Monthly and is currently an England
Selector.

CONTENTS

INTRODUCTION 6

SHORE FISHING 8

PIER FISHING 36

BOAT FISHING 58

LURE FISHING 92

BAITS 102

TACKLE 118

FISH 142

CONCLUSION 160

INTRODUCTION

Anyone can go shore fishing. There are no licences required and it doesn't cost a lot of money. All that's needed is rod and reel, a packet of bait and with thousands of miles of shoreline to explore it's no wonder that fishing is still the UK's biggest participation sport. Shore fishing around the UK can be very rewarding, but requires a different approach depending on the part of the country and the style of coastline. Some areas with shallow shingle beaches may require long casts to reach the fish, while at other marks the fish can literally be under your feet. Tackle need not be expensive, but you tend to get what you pay for. A cheap rod will catch fish, but may not cast as far as an expensive one that will have better rod rings and a longer lasting reel seat. Nevertheless, beginners won't notice the difference to start with, and it's more important to get the right type of rod for the area being fished and the correct bait.

SHORE
FISHING

SHORE FISHING

TACKLE AND BAIT

If you are targeting fish like pollack, garfish and mackerel, a lightweight rod and float rig will give you good sport. Use a sand eel or mackerel strip for bait, or cast a lure or spinner for some more active sport. For wrasse and codling you will need a rod and reel with a bit more power to get the fish out of the rocks. Peeler crab, ragworm and lugworm are best bait-fished on a paternoster rig for this type of fishing. Bottom species, such as ray and huss, can be caught on regular beach casting tackle provided the bottom is not too rough. A running leger with mackerel or squid strip will pick up most bottom species.

LEADER LINE

As most shore fishing requires the ability to cast, it needs the angler to be careful not to injure any member of the public, as a fast moving lead weight is a deadly missile. To take the strain of that first power surge as the lead is cast out to sea, a leader line of at least 5 metres should be attached to the main line. The main line on the reel is usually between 15 lb to 20 lb breaking strain and the leader should be at least 30 lb. For really long distance casting this should be stepped up to around 50lb as the power developed during a pendulum cast, for instance, is awesome. The heavier leader line will also absorb a lot of the abrasion from the sand or shingle as the line is retrieved.

🐟 **Always use a leader line when casting from the shore.**

CASTING

We all admire someone who can cast out long distances, but don't become blinkered in thinking the fish are only found a long way out. The most natural feeding areas for sea fish are along the tide line where the shingle meets the sand, or in the gully at the bottom of the beach; it's quite easy to cast over good fish. Bass are a very good example of a species that love to come very close inshore to find crab and shellfish washed out by the waves. Accurate casting is more important, and a walk along the beach at low tide will reveal where the natural bait holding areas are. These can be paced out to the high tide mark so a cast can be made into these areas when the tide comes in.

Casting developments

In the casting world things have turned a full circle. Overhead casting was the way to cast until the late seventies, and when looking for ways to get their bait out further, a method called pendulum casting became the vogue. This involves standing with your back to the sea with the lead hanging on a drop of around nine feet, or just level with the reel. The lead is then swung back towards land, then towards the sea behind your back, before turning and pulling the lead right round the body and out to sea. This produced a massive momentum and the first casts of over 200 yards were achieved. Special stiffer rods were developed to cope with this style, and distances rose as a result. What was sometimes lost, however, was the sensitivity of the rod tip, and a few years ago anglers began to look for an alternative. They found it by using much longer rods, as used by continental anglers, complete with a large fixed spool reel loaded with braided line. While being too long to pendulum, with the extra length and softer tip, really long overhead casts can be achieved. Some of these rods are as long as 5 metres, very often telescopic for easy transport.

TAKE ADVICE

When looking to buy a shore rod be aware of what you want, as some rods will be great on the field for casting, others will be heavy rods for cod fishing, but if you are after flounders in an estuary a different style of rod will be required. Always explain to the tackle dealer where you intend to fish, what fish you are after and what style of casting you are capable of, so they can guide you to the right choice.

RIGS

The end tackle does not need to be too complicated for shore fishing as long as the bait is presented well and cast to the right spot. A simple paternoster with a couple of hooks above the weight is the most efficient way to get the bait out for most fish. If bigger fish are the target then a single hook with a running leger and baited with peeler crab or fish bait would be best. Generally speaking the body of the trace should be as strong as the leader line otherwise it will break during the cast. The hook lengths or snoods as they are sometimes known can be finer depending on the species targeted. If one of the hooks becomes snagged this can then be broken free, and so saving the rest of the tackle.

Clipped rigs

Where long casts are required it makes sense to use a clipped rig. This is where the baited hooks, snoods are clipped over a metal or plastic clip that holds it under tension to make the rig aerodynamic. When the lead hits the water the tension is released and the hooks come off the clips to fish naturally. There are several different methods that release the clips: one of the most popular is the impact lead that has a plastic top to the lead that is pushed up as it hits the water and releases the hooks. Rigs can be clipped up or clipped down, and in some cases they go up over one clip and down to another allowing a longer hook length to be used.

ELASTIC COTTON

Many anglers complain that they catch less fish than other people using the same bait, and this could be because uneven casting is affecting the bait. Some soft bait can easily be damaged during the cast, so it's a good idea to use bait elastic to hold them on the hook. Mackerel strip can be whipped onto the shank with several turns of elastic or whipped up to resemble a small sausage before putting it on the hook. This can then be slid up the hook to create an attractive bait. Peeler crab is another bait that needs to be whipped on to be sure it arrives on the seabed in perfect condition. As we can never see what condition our baits arrive in, a good experiment is to try a baited cast at low tide or in a local field to see what the bait looks like after a cast. If a casting style is too jerky this will be revealed if the bait is hanging off the hooks or missing altogether.

🐟 **Bait elastic can help get the bait out in top condition.**

SLIDING TACKLE

Match anglers are always ready to use clever tactics to catch their fish, and through the summer many will use a sliding hook to catch a few extra fish such as mackerel, garfish and scad. A two-hook rig is cast out with a fixed grapnel or breakaway lead on, and an extra hook attached to a float is clipped onto the main line and slid down the line by holding the rod up high. This lets the free running float and hook slide down to the water where it will gradually work its way further out to sea. This is a good way to catch both the bottom feeding fish and those that swim in the upper layers of the sea — like mackerel, garfish and scad — at the same time.

🐟 **An extra hook can be slid down the line for fish feeding near the surface.**

CHECK IT OUT

It pays to check out a beach at low tide before you fish it. This will show where there are any obstructions, rocks, gullies or anything else that can hold fish or be a potential spot tackle could be lost on. It's sometimes worth making a quick sketch of the beach and marking the likely fish holding spots. Pace out the distances they are from the high tide mark as the beach will look so different when the tide comes in later. It's putting in the extra bit of effort and giving yourself a bit more knowledge that pays off, rather than the 'chuck it and see' style of angling many people adopt. Another thing with less experienced shore anglers is to fish the nearest point to where the car is parked. The more successful angler is prepared to take a ten-minute walk along the beach to a spot away from everyone else.

COLLECTING BAIT

One of the joys of shore fishing is getting to the beach at low tide and searching for the natural baits on the beach that day. Always look for shellfish washed up by heavy seas. If there are slipper limpets, razor fish or cockles blown up on the beach the fish will move in to feed on them as the tide comes in. Lugworm can be dug with a spade or pumped up with a bait pump, whereas ragworm are best dug with a fork. If there are rock pools, try using a small net to catch prawns or look for crabs hiding in the rocks. All these will catch fish and collecting them satisfies the hunter-gatherer instincts that all anglers possess.

🐟 Always check along the beach for natural baits that have been washed up.

BUYING BAIT

Although there is a great satisfaction in collecting your own bait, most people have limited time or live far from the beach so buying it is the only option. It is often best to phone and book bait, as tackle shops can only keep a limited amount of live bait otherwise the only option will be frozen. Live bait such as peeler crab, lugworm, ragworm and sand eels are by far the best, but some frozen bait will catch fish regularly. Squid and mackerel freeze down well and are excellent while worm baits are not so successful. Frozen hermit crabs can often out-fish the fresh ones. It is crucial to get the very best bait as it's the only bit the fish is interested in. An expensive rod, flashy reel and beautifully made tackle with beads and sequins won't catch fish; it's the bait that goes on the hook that catches them.

🐟 It's the bait that catches the fish not the equipment.

BITES

One of the most frequent questions newcomers to shore fishing want to know is, "How will I know if I have a bite?". In fact it's quite easy to tell the difference between the regular action of the waves as they pull down on the line from the rat-a-tat of a fish bite. Even small fish will make the rod tip rattle, and bigger fish will thump the tip down really hard. The more difficult thing is deciding if the fish is hooked, or merely sampling the bait. With fish like bass, codling, smooth hound and whiting, once they have the bait they keep pulling on the rod and it's just a case of picking up the rod and winding into them. Keep the line coming in steadily and don't allow slack line to form as that's when fish get off. When fishing for flounders and other flatfish it is best to allow a little time after seeing the first bite for the fish to get the bait down. Sometimes there is no more indication after that first bite that a fish is on, as it may have settled into the sand; wait a minute or two them wind in. You will soon be aware if there is a fish on or not as it will feel heavier than just the lead weight. Another classic bite is the slack liner. What this could mean is a fish has picked up the bait and has continued swimming inshore unaware it's hooked and looking for more food. Wind in quickly to catch up with the fish, and as soon as weight on the line is felt lift the rod up to set the hook as you continue winding in.

🐟 **With many bites it's just a matter of lifting the rod to hook the fish.**

GRIP LEADS

One of the most important items a shore angler needs is a grip lead to anchor the bait on the bottom. Powerful tides or strong winds can sweep the tackle along the beach, so it's important to counteract this by using the right weight. Grip leads come in two basic types: the fixed grapnel or the breakaway. For extreme conditions the grapnel is the answer as it is the most efficient at keeping a grip on the bottom; when it's time to retrieve it the wires will bend out under pressure. The more widely used breakaway is the perfect combination of a weight that will hold the bottom, but release easily when required. The weight is designed with wires that are pushed into a groove when set to grip that spring free when the rod is pulled. Plain lead weights can be used where there is little tide, or if the bait is required to be moved along with the tide to seek out the fish. If using rigs with the hooks clipped up or down you need to buy the suitable weight that will often incorporate a release mechanism that will ensure the hooks come free on contact with the water.

🐟 **In extreme conditions a fixed grapnel will keep the bait out there.**

ROCK FISHING

All fishing is fun, but it can turn to disaster if the correct precautions are not taken and the wrong equipment used; rock fishing is a good example. Some of the best shore fishing is in the most inaccessible places that involve climbing down steep banks, across boulders or down rocky slopes. The rewards can be codling, wrasse, pollack, ray, huss, conger as well as garfish, scad and mackerel. Don't go alone to these types of marks, and make sure someone at home knows where you intend to fish and when you are due back. Wear suitable footwear and it may be advisable to carry a rope for the steeper slopes. Check the tides to see that you won't be cut off as it rises and take care when casting on slippery rocks. A lightweight lifejacket should not be out of the question in the more precarious spots. Tackle may need to be on the heavy side if fishing high cliffs such as Filey Brig, where decent fish need to be wound up the cliffs. In some areas of the South West lightweight spinning or float gear will catch plenty of fish.

🐟 **Don't go alone when fishing dangerous rocky marks.**

SHINGLE BEACHES

There are many shingle beaches along the east and south coasts in particular. These can be divided up into shallow tidal areas where hundreds of yards of sand are exposed at low tide, and steeply shelving ones that are always deep enough to fish whatever the state of tide. It's important to check the tide tables when fishing shallow beaches as there may be several hours when there's not enough water to fish. Generally they are fishable from three hours before high tide on the flood, then another three hours on the ebb. It may be that longish casts are required to get to the fish so check this out when buying bait from the local tackle shop. The steeply shelving beaches such as Deal, Sandgate, Dungeness, Langney Point and Chesil Beach can be fished at any time but be careful on the shingle in rough weather as there can be a strong undertow making the beach near the sea unstable. Long casts are not neccesary on these beaches as the fish will move in to feed in the gullies at the bottom of the beach.

🐟 Steep shingle beaches can have a dangerous undertow.

ESTUARIES

Fishing in estuaries presents a few different opportunities for anglers. For a start, there are sometimes strong tides and often the water is a mixture of salt and fresh water; this means the species found here are the ones that can adapt to these conditions. Bass, mullet and flounders are the particular ones that can cope with less salinity but there are others; thornback ray are found in many estuaries in the south west and are often caught on prawns. In Ireland the Shannon estuary produces rays, bull huss and tope for shore anglers. In recent years, with global warming increasing the sea temperature, gilthead bream have been caught in many estuaries. Casting is not the way to success in estuaries: it's finding the gullies and pools where the food gathers, and putting the right bait into these spots. An estuary can be an ideal place to fish when it's too rough to fish the open beach as there is usually plenty of shelter.

OTHER EQUIPMENT

Although shore fishing can be done cheaply with a minimum of equipment, there are some items that make life a lot easier and the fishing more comfortable, especially in poor conditions. A rod rest is a must, as standing holding a rod all day becomes a chore. A decent tripod will make a firm rod rest for nearly all types of shoreline, even on the rocks. Don't set the rod tip too high as it can hurt the neck looking up in the air for several hours. Another item that will serve several purposes is a Beach Buddy. These are an easy to erect tent, on an aluminium frame, that are very stable. They not only serve as a windbreak or a sun shade, they can be used to keep food and tackle dry and the sun off the bait. A cool box is another extra that can be crucial on a warm day for keeping bait in tip-top condition.

🐟 **In calm conditions the rod tip can be kept low to avoid neck ache.**

LAMPS

Night time is probably the best time to fish from the shore as the fish feel more confident moving into shallow water to feed. This means having suitable lighting: either a lamp to light an area around you, or a good quality headlamp. There was a time when pressure lamps were a must on the beach but modern headlamps with their Halogen bulbs are so efficient that many anglers now rely on these for all their lighting. Make sure the tip of the rod has some reflective tape or paint on so it will show up well when a light is directed at it. Be careful not to direct the beam into other anglers eyes when using a powerful halogen lamp as it can leave them with night blindness for several minutes.

🐟 Use some reflective tape on the rod tip for night fishing.

MAINTENANCE

To get the best out of your fishing gear it needs looking after as salt water is so damaging if not washed off after a fishing session. It's easy to come back from a trip and dump the gear in the garage while you rush indoors to show off your catch or prepare it for cooking. By the following weekend, when the tackle is needed again, it will be showing signs of neglect.

🐟 Always find time to wipe off rods and reels with fresh water to remove salt deposits.

🐟 A spray of WD40 will prevent any harm coming to the metal parts such as the rod rings and reel seat.

🐟 Always check the top eye of the rod before they are put away, especially if the rods have been put in and out of the car, as these are so susceptible to damage. It's not the time to find one broken next time you get on the beach.

🐟 Check the first 20 metres of your line as it may be suffering from abrasion after being dragged through sand or rocks, and discard it if showing signs of wear.

CARE OF FISH

It's inevitable while shore fishing that some of the fish caught will be very small, undersized or unwanted. As concerned anglers we need to get these fish back in the water so they can survive and unhooking them and tossing them casually back in the sea doesn't give them much chance. The trauma of being pulled from the sea and the shock of hitting the surface when returned stuns the fish and makes them vunerable to predators such as seagulls, bass and crabs. A better way to deal with them is to gently put them in a bucket of seawater and in a few minutes they will be ready to slip back into the sea. This is known to increase the survival rate by a big margin.

🐟 **Keep small fish in a bucket for a while before returning them to the sea.**

KEEPING FISH

Keeping fish for the pot is fine providing the minimum size limits are adhered to. The NFSA produces a list of the minimum sizes and for a fish to be suitable for the table it should be well above these recommended sizes. Any fish to be kept should be dispatched with a sharp blow to the head with a priest or a lead weight rather than leaving them flapping about in a bucket. A cool box with some ice in will keep your catch fresh until it can be eaten, put in the fridge or frozen down. It's a good idea to gut your fish before you leave the beach; the remains can be thrown into the sea where they will soon be cleared up by seagulls, crabs and shrimps. Trying to get rid of smelly fish remains when you get home, especially now most areas only have fortnightly bin collections, can give rise to upsets with family and neighbours.

🐟 If fish are being retained clean them before you leave the beach.

NURSERY AREAS

Check for any restrictions such as bass nursery areas, with the local tackle shop when buying your bait. It's illegal to fish these areas so make sure you know where they are and avoid them. Always remember, these restricted areas where the small fish are allowed to grow without having to avoid nets, are good for the angler. The result will be more and hopefully better quality fish for the future. Many harbours and marinas don't allow fishing in the close proximity of moored boats but have areas where fishing is allowed.

🐟 Don't fish in bass nursery areas they are preserving our future stocks.

TIDES

Success at shore fishing relies heavily on fishing the best part of the tide, and this can be completely different in different areas. The tides are also vital for bait collecting and for knowing when to move off sand banks or rocky marks as the tide begins to come in. In some places the tide will flood faster than walking pace, and every year anglers get trapped by the incoming tide. Generally the fishing is best on the rising tide, but this is not the complete picture. Some times low tide can allow shore anglers to cast to gullies that cannot be reached at high tide. Many shallow beaches will only produce fish over a two-hour period of high tide. Once again ask at the local tackle shop or other anglers for advice.

🐟 **Knowing the tides can be vital to the fishing and your safety.**

NEW MARKS

One of the most satisfying things for shore anglers is seeking out new marks. To tackle a new venue means using a bit of common sense. If it's a shallow sandy bay then the likelihood is the fish will stay well out in daylight requiring long casts to catch them. On any mark the clearer the water the less likely the fish will come inshore until dark, except heavily weeded areas where the fish have some cover.

Off a steep shingle bank, with deep, coloured water and a bit of tide, the fish are likely to feed throughout the day and long casts may not be neccesary.

Check out the tides before tackling somewhere new as anglers get stranded every year by not knowing how quickly the tide comes in. Make sure you have a good idea of an exit route if fishing from rocks, as water can fill in gullies behind you as the tide rises. The same can be said when fishing at low tide at night. Water can come in very quickly on shallow beaches and if it becomes misty as well it's easy to become disorientated.

🐟 Always have a planned exit route when fishing from rocky marks.

COMPETITIONS

Shore anglers have a host of competitions: they can fish at club level, local festivals, big open events and national leagues. It's a great world to get into and a good way to learn all the latest techniques as many events are pegged, and the next angler could be the local champion or an international. Clubs run regular competitions for a few hours in the evening and occasional weekend matches, and have trophies for the best of each species each year. These are very relaxed affairs: still competitive but not so intense as a league match for example. Open competitions attract anglers from a wide area with some big prizes to be won. Many are pegged, meaning you draw a number and have to fish from that spot all day. If it's a zoned match you will be able to fish in a certain area and not tied down to one peg. Other matches can be roving, especially where the biggest fish will take the top prize, such as a 'cod only' match.

PREPARATION

To be successful in competitions you need to put in some preparation. This means tying several rigs suitable for the species caught in that area, as snags and snap offs can occur at anytime and having spare rigs ready is important. The rules may allow you to have spare baited traces ready for the next cast. These can be hung on you tripod so they can easily be clipped on when you retrieve your tackle. Make sure your leader line is in good condition and the reel is running smoothly, and have a spare rod with you so you don't waste time if there is a problem with your other one. Make sure you read the rules thoroughly as competitions are run in several different ways: you may have to fish to local or national size limits and take all the fish back to a weigh-in. Many matches nowadays are 'Catch & Release': this means recording each fish on a match card with the angler next to you signing your card, then returning the fish to the sea. Check what the tide is doing, so you can cast to allow for the current pushing your line along the beach. Make sure you plan what bait you will need and collect or order it in good time.

LEAGUES

The shore leagues started in earnest in the late 70's and are now very much part of the angling scene. At the beginning of the 80's the various leagues got together and formed the National Sea League, with qualifiers from each league meeting for a big final. About this time the Sea Anglers Match Federation was formed to put together a set of rules that all matches could be fished to where cash prizes were involved. They also created a series of matches from which members could qualify for the SAMF Masters final with a big cash prize for the winner. These leagues are still running in most areas of the UK. Your local tackle shop should be able to put you in touch with the organisers if you want to give it a go.

BASS FISHING

There's no doubt the most cherished and sought after fish for the shore angler is the mighty bass. They are a spectacular looking fish with large silvery scales, aggressive spiky dorsal fins and most of all they grow large. Another important feature for the shore angler is that they give a really good fight once they are hooked and can be caught very close to shore. On sandy beaches after a gale they will come in close to pick up worms and shellfish washed out by the surf. In these circumstances casts should be made to around the third wave out — a cast anyone should be able to achieve. Baits should be black lugworm or any shellfish washed up onshore, as this is what the bass will be looking for. In rocky areas bass can be caught even closer to shore as they follow the tide in through the gullies between the rocks while searching for prawns, crabs and small fish. Again the choice of bait should be the same as the things they are hunting for. On piers and breakwaters bass will feed close to the piles, looking for prawns and heads and guts of mackerel thrown over by anglers. Late summer each year when the bass have become used to this free feed of mackerel heads those anglers confident enough to fish with a big mackerel bait land some seriously large bass.

COD FISHING

In the south of the country cod fishing from the shore is generally restricted to the winter months, but the further north you go the season extends out to cover most of the year. The top two baits for

shore-caught cod are peeler crab and lugworm.
Squid comes next, especially when it's used to tip
off a lugworm bait. The best time to land a codling
on the shallow sandy beaches is at night when they
venture closer inshore. Daytime fishing requires
long casts as the fish stay well out until darkness
falls. The only exception to this is after a gale
when the water is stirred up and they feel safer in
the poorer visibility. On rocky coasts the cod will
happily feed during the day in amongst the weed,
searching out crabs and prawns. Although cod don't
fight quite as spectacularly as bass, they have
plenty of bulk and their head shaking action will
test out tackle if it's not up to the job.

Here are some noted shore fishing marks from
different parts of the country worth a try. We
suggest the best baits and what species there are
to be caught.

Silloth, Cumbria

The town of Silloth in Cumbria is renowned by
shore anglers for its shallow beach, long wooden
groynes and its flounders. There are other species
to catch — notably plaice, mullet and bass — but
it's the flounders that bring most anglers to the
area. Best bait by far is peeler crab as the
flounders move in during early spring to feast on
the shore crabs when they emerge from their old
shells. Other bait such as lugworm and ragworm
will catch fish, but are stripped by crabs within
minutes of being cast out. This is a spring and
summer mark and fishing is best a couple of hours
either side of low tide.

Rossall Point, Lancashire

Just north of Fleetwood is the shore venue of Rossall Point. During the autumn and winter there are plenty of cod and whiting to be caught. Fishing over the low tide puts the bait into some rough ground where a lugworm or crab bait will soon be taken. The venue can be fished at high tide but night is the best time to try through the summer for bass, flounder and eels.

River Mersey, Merseyside

There are several marks along the Mersey where good catches can be made, but they are all governed by the fast flowing current. Grip leads are necessary to anchor the bait out into the river. Some of the marks are fished from breakwaters: such as Seaforth, the promenade at Otterspool and the beaches of Vale Park and Perch Rock beach. Generally the best time to fish is over the low or high tides when the tides are slackest, particularly when they occur as it gets dark. Lugworm, ragworm and crab are top baits, but put on several worms if that's your choice as they wash out quickly in the tide or soon get stripped by crabs.

Colwyn Bay, North Wales

The Promenade at Colwyn Bay is a safe and convenient place to fish, with railing and easy parking close at hand. Fishing is best a few hours either side of high tide and through the summer plaice, bass, dogfish and mackerel feature in the catches. Winter sees a good run of whiting and codling taken with catches improving in the dark. Best baits are lugworm, ragworm and mackerel, with sand eel a good alternative.

The Mumbles, South Wales

Another safe and convenient shore venue is Knab Rock, a few miles east from the Mumbles. Fishing is from a concrete esplanade with handy railings for resting the rods on, and the car can be parked close to the fishing spot. Baiting with lugworm, ragworm, mackerel, squid or crab will produce a good range of species such as bass, plaice, mackerel, trigger fish and garfish, plus all sorts of others from the mainly clean ground. As with most marks in winter, the whiting and codling dominate catches.

Seaton, Devon

Fishing at Seaton is from a fairly steep shingle beach where casts of around 100 yards will put the bait out far enough for a good range of species. In season you will find bass, ray, dogfish, pollack, mackerel and garfish, with the codling starting in late autumn. Best baits are mackerel, squid, peeler crab and lugworm, with sand eels a particular local favourite, whether live or frozen.

Brixham, Devon

The Breakwater at Brixham stretches well out to sea and makes an excellent fishing mark provided it isn't too rough. Near the lighthouse at the end of the breakwater it gets very busy in the summer months, with anglers chasing the mackerel shoals with feathers and others float fishing for garfish. Along the outer edge produces some quality fish with conger, bass, wrasse, plaice and pollack all taken regularly. For fishing the bottom use fish baits or have fun with a float rig for mackerel, bass, pollack and garfish baited with sand eel or a strip of mackerel. This type of fishing is always a lot of fun as you watch the float, waiting for it to dive straight under.

St Catherine's Breakwater, Jersey

One of the most famous marks in the Channel Islands is St Catherine's breakwater where some truly remarkable fish have been landed, including more than one British record. The solid concrete breakwater is over half a mile long and can accommodate a large number of anglers. Because of the strong tides it's best to fish over the slack tides an hour or so before and after low water, and the same at high water. Fairly strong tackle is required coupled with a fairly powerful beachcaster. Baits should be decent sized fillets of mackerel or squid that will catch ray, bass, huss and small congers, while smaller rigs baited with squid will catch bream and other smaller species. Near the breakwater a crab bait or a ragworm can pick up some very large wrasse.

Chesil Beach, Dorset

The 18-mile stretch of shingle stretching from Weymouth to West Bay is world famous. For the angler it is an awesome place to fish. The steep shingle bank needs to be treated with respect as the undertow can draw out masses of shingle from under your feet when there is a sea running, so care is needed. Difficult to fish in a south westerly, it comes into its own when it settles down after a blow. Night is the other time to get the best out of Chesil beach. The deep end is from Portland to Abbotsbury, getting shallower through West

Bexington and further on. Masses of mackerel and
garfish move in through the summer months but in
late summer all sorts of fish appear; triggerfish,
bream, codling, plaice, whiting, gurnard, dogfish
and smoothhound can all be taken during a single
session in the right conditions. Best bait is a
ragworm and squid combo, lugworm tipped with
squid, or mackerel fillet, peeler crab and frozen
sand eel. The further west you go the shallower
the beach becomes so longer casts are required,
but there's a greater chance of catching big plaice.

Chale, Isle of Wight
There are not many places where sea anglers have
a chance of catching ray from the shore. Chale bay
on the due south of the island is one of those
places where ray are caught each year through the
summer months. The shingle beach with a backdrop
of cliffs needs to be fished when the sea has been
stirred up by a bit of a blow. Best bait is sand eel,
either fresh or frozen with mackerel strip an
alternative. The ground is broken so keep the rig
simple using a single 3/0 hook on a short running
leger.

Lee-on-Solent, Hampshire
Over a mile of gently sloping shingle beaches
interspersed with wooden groynes make this venue,
just west of Gosport, a favourite mark. Those
people fishing a few hours either side of high tide
will find plaice, smoothhound, bass, ray and
dogfish in the summer months, along with mackerel
shoals on calm warm evenings. Fishing improves
with darkness, while winter fishing produces

whiting, pout and flounders. Ragworm, crab, mackerel and squid are the best baits to use in the Solent during the summer, with lugworm working best in the winter months.

Reculver, Kent
No chance of missing this venue with the twin peaks of the Reculver towers a prominent landmark. Large catches of whiting are made in the winter along with some quality cod; black lugworm and crab are the best baits. During the spring and summer there is a chance of a thornback ray or smoothhound along with eels, flounder and bass; peeler crab is by far the best option for bait.

Orford Ness, Suffolk
Like the famous Dover Breakwater you need to take a boat to fish from Orford Ness. They run a ferry service from the village of Orford each morning and late afternoon. This extraordinary venue is similar to Chesil beach in Dorset in the fact it is a wide shingle bank that allows fishing into deep water without the need for long casting. Considered to be one of the best cod marks in the country, it also fishes well in the summer for bass, sole, pout, eel and smooth hound with all sorts of other species likely to turn up. The sole take lugworm but use peeler crab for anything else. In winter take plenty of lugworm for the cod with a bit of squid to tip off the baits with. Take care when landing a decent fish as the shingle is very steep and an undertow can occur in rough conditions.

Seaham, County Durham

There are two famous marks at Seaham, the Blast and Chemical beaches. Both were soiled by the coal industry, as the names suggest, but the seawater coloured by coal dust made the cod bolder and they could be caught in good numbers and fairly close in. Since the demise of the coal industry the beaches and the water are much cleaner and this has changed the fishing. More whiting and flatfish can now be caught, while the cod are still there, but stay further out in daylight. At night the cod catches improve considerably, best baits being ragworm and lugworm.

PIER
FISHING

PIER FISHING

Why is pier fishing so popular? Firstly, it allows shore anglers with little experience to be able to get a line far enough out to sea to catch fish. Generally it's a safe environment with plenty of other anglers around, so it's socially a lot of fun. Piers come in all shapes and sizes, with structures made with wooden piles, metal girders, concrete blocks or granite rocks. They can be up to a mile long or just poking a few metres out to sea, but they all give the opportunity for anglers to cast into deep water where the chance of catching fish is much better. It gives juniors an opportunity to catch fish with fairly cheap tackle, and after landing their first one are often hooked for life.

EASY FISHING

Although more than half the piers built in Victorian times have been lost to storm damage, fire and other misfortunes like ships colliding with them — and in one instance a mine blowing it up — there are still nearly 50 spread around the UK coastline. For many sea anglers their first experience of wetting a line will be at a young age dangling a line off the local pier. With the development of marinas in recent years the concrete arms have provided more access points for anglers to fish from. The main reason so many young anglers start on the pier is because good fishing can be had without the need to cast too far. In fact many of the best fish taken from piers and marinas are found within a few yards of the supports or the concrete base. This is because small fish, crabs and prawns all gather here for safety and the larger fish patrol the structure looking for an opportunity to grab anything that has strayed away from its shelter.

🦈 **Many of the best fish are caught within a few yards of the base of the pier.**

COSTS

Nearly all piers charge a fee for fishing. Sometimes it is charged per person, while other pier owners will charge per rod; generally the cost for fishing will range from £1 to £5 for the day. Many have regular security patrols and a few are closed to anglers during stormy weather, so check before you set out that the pier is open to fishing.

SKILLS

Pier fishing should not be regarded as just a starting point for junior anglers, as many different skills are required for the different fish that arrive through the seasons. While summer fishing is probably the most popular, especially through the long summer holidays, many senior anglers can't wait for the autumn when there are less holidaymakers on the pier, and the whiting and codling begin to show. Summer fish such as mullet, garfish and bass are species that need special attention to detail, and no little skill to catch regularly off piers, with the right tackle and bait being of particular importance. Mackerel can arrive in vast shoals and things can get a little hectic with dozens of anglers all casting sets of lures towards the shoal. Anglers targeting mullet use very light tackle, bait with bread and use ground bait to bring the fish on the feed. Some areas have some excellent flatfish within easy casting distance, with dabs and plaice during the day and a possibility of a much sought after sole during the hours of darkness.

🐟 Things can get a little hectic when the mackerel shoals arrive.

TACKLE

More or less any shore casting or spinning rod can be used off a pier. In some areas, such as the north east, a more powerful rod with a medium sized multiplier is required, as the main target will be cod. In summer months a light spinning rod matched to a fixed spool reel can give the angler some excellent sport. The spinning rod will be ideal for float fishing garfish, mackerel, bass and pollack where long casts are not required but more accuracy is needed. For bottom fishing, where a longer cast will get to the better fish, a longer rod of up to 12 ft and a multiplier reel is probably the best bet. Always take the time to ask at the local tackle shop about rigs, tackle and what fish are about, when collecting your bait, as they will be only too pleased to advise which set-up is best.

FLOATS

A fairly large float can be used from a pier as long as it's weighted correctly. This can then be cast with some degree of accuracy to areas, such as close to girders or supports, where many fish lurk. Alternatively, it can be allowed to drift out on the tide away from the pier to where the predatory fish patrol. The use of the float is primarily to present a bait, especially a live bait, off the bottom, so it appears in a natural state. It also keeps the bait out of the way of crabs that can destroy a legered bait in minutes.

Use a sliding float with a stop knot so the depth can be changed easily to search out where the shoals of fish are feeding. There are two other sorts of float that can be used with good effect from a pier. The first is a bubble float that can be half filled with water; this makes it heavy enough to cast quite good distances and with a little more or less water can be made to float enough to be seen clearly. There is another float that is self-weighted. This one has some lead inside the float and makes it easy to cast; it will stand upright without any other weight required, but a swan shot needs to be added to the trace to ensure the bait drops slowly to the preset depth.

BAITS

Just about any bait can be used off a pier. All worm baits work well – lugworm, ragworm and white rag are good for a wide range of species. Lugworm is a good bait for codling, whiting and flatfish, while ragworm will pick out the wrasse, pollack and sole at night. White ragworm are the match angler's favourite, as they will catch most species including smooth hound. Peeler crab and hermit crab are a bit more specialised but if there are smooth hound and bass around, these are the baits to catch them. It may be necessary to fix the crab on the hook with elastic cotton. Fish baits such as mackerel and squid will catch cod, bass and even conger eels from some areas. Float fishing allows the use of some baits that are more difficult to use off the shore such as live sand eel and live prawns. The float should be allowed to drift in close to the pier so the bait is near the piles, or the side if you are on a breakwater, as that's where fish expect to find prawns and crabs.

LANDING FISH

One of the biggest problems fishing from a pier or harbour arm is landing the fish, especially a decent one. Lifting a heavy fish up the side will usually result in the line breaking and the fish lost. The experienced pier angler will always carry a drop net. This is a large net about the circumference of a bicycle wheel, with a sturdy line attached, that can be lowered into the water. The net should be lowered to just below the surface so the fish can be guided over it and gently lifted to engulf the fish so it can be pulled onto the pier. For smaller fish, provided a decent leader line is added to the main line, can be wound up, hand lined or even swung up to safety.

Best way to land big fish is with a drop net.

TIDES

To fish a pier successfully means fishing at the right time of the tide: some piers dry out over the low tide or have very little water to fish in. Organise your trip to include the high tide, when the water will be at its deepest and the fish have had time to come in. Also the direction of the tide is very important for deciding which side to fish. For fishing on the bottom it's best to fish on the down side of the pier with the tide going away from you. If the intention is to let a prawn or a white ragworm float under the pier for bass or pollack then the uptide side, with the tide running towards you, is the place to be. The better fishing inshore is always on the bigger or spring tides, but strong tides can be encountered on some breakwaters and the longer piers.

GROUND BAITING

Where there are good shoals of mullet, it can increase catches terrifically if a bag of ground bait is used. Something like an onion sack filled with bread crumbs mixed with some old fish or fish oil and lowered down to hang just touching the surface will send out a scent trail, and start the fish feeding. Then drop a hook baited with bread or a small piece of mackerel flesh amongst the trail of bits coming from the bag, and be ready for action. If the bag is filled with just fish bait, all crushed up, this will attract mackerel, pollack and garfish. Another method of ground baiting from a pier is to use a small bait dropper below a float. This allows a trickle of scent to flow out close to the bait and draw the fish in. There are weights available that incorporate a swim feeder fixed on the shaft for bottom fishing. Fish like bream and whiting can be attracted to this method if crushed mackerel, herring or lugworm is put into the swim feeder.

🐟 **Ground baiting can bring the mullet on the feed.**

SAFETY

With the modern trend to seemingly ban anything that could constitute a slight danger, and Health and Safety sometimes being taken to rather extreme lengths, many piers have either banned fishing or restricted them to small areas away from the general public. It is every angler's responsibility to take care when casting, as a lead weight can be a dangerous missile if misdirected or breaking off during the power surge. This is why a strong leader line is advised to help prevent a snap-off occurring. Some piers only allow underarm casting, or even no casting at all, but there are always fish to be caught close in. Don't try fancy casting from a pier: a straight overhead cast, if permitted, will get the line far enough to catch most fish. Keep the area around you clear of any fish heads, bait or baited tackle, as people could slip. Be particularly careful with spare baited traces as a dog could easily pick up one of them with tragic consequences.

SEASONS

Throughout the summer holidays the piers are extra busy and generally the more experienced anglers avoid them during this period. At this time of the year most anglers will be trying for mackerel or garfish, as these are probably the most obliging of fish taking either lures or thin strips of fish bait. The bass and mullet are there as well but need specialist tactics to catch. Other summer fish such as pout, wrasse, coalfish and pollack can be caught right next to the pier. In the autumn the first of the whiting move in with the dabs and sole at dusk. Some of the bigger bass are caught in the autumn using mackerel heads fished close to the pier. Then as winter approaches the codling arrive and stay through to the spring in many areas. This is when the keen pier anglers can be found as the rewards can be well worth the effort. Springtime brings smoothhound to many areas and these can make exciting fishing using peeler or hermit crab as bait. Plaice also move back in during spring, after spawning in deep water, and although a bit thin can be caught on some piers in good numbers.

🐟 **Try mackerel heads for the big bass.**

POLARISED SUNGLASSES

Being able to see fish in the water can assist greatly when fishing from a pier and polarised sunglasses help in this. The glare from the surface of the sea prevents the eye seeing down into the water, but with polarised glasses all is revealed.

It's possible to see a shoal of mullet swimming close to the pier, for example, while to other people, without polarised glasses, they are invisible. The rays from the sun can be very damaging so a good quality pair of sunglasses is a must as most of the time is spent gazing down at the water.

🐟 Protect your eyes with a pair of properly polarised sunglasses.

COOL BOX

It can get very warm on a pier during the summer so a small cool box will be needed to keep the bait from getting too warm. As stated before, the one thing with any fishing that needs to be right is the quality of bait. Many anglers will make the effort to travel to the mark carrying all sorts of tackle and equipment, but scrimp on the bait. Or worse still some people buy decent bait only to leave it in the sun and find it's useless after a couple of hours. Don't put bait like ragworm directly against a freezer block as the iced block will kill them: wrap your freezer blocks in newspaper and they will stay cool for much longer and not harm the bait.

🐟 Use a cool box to keep bait fresh.

NIGHT FISHING

If your local pier allows fishing at night, or even into dusk, the catches will improve dramatically. After a day trying for mackerel or garfish on the float switch over to bottom fishing as a host of species will be moving in to patrol close into the pier. Soles become active as darkness falls and shoals of pout will take nearly any bait they find. One species that doesn't feed at night is the wrasse; as soon as dusk arrives they stop feeding. Cod fishing is far better in the dark, while fish like smooth hound and dogfish use their highly developed sense of smell to find their food. Conger eels will also be moving out of their hidey holes to forage around the pier for small fish, crabs and anything live caught away from shelter. To target the conger a strong trace of 60lb to 100lb mono is required. Baits need to be any fresh fish such as mackerel, garfish or pout, as congers prefer fresh or live bait to anything else. Another species that can be caught in darkness are big bass that will be looking for any heads or guts thrown over earlier in the day.

RESTRICTIONS

All piers and marinas are owned by someone, be it the local council or a private company, and they will have certain restrictions for anglers. In some places there will no fishing allowed while in others all fishing must cease at certain times. Another rule on many piers is that only underarm casting is allowed due to the general public being in close proximity. On many piers there will be a charge for each rod used and on others it will be a charge per angler. Attention must be paid to these different restrictions as the irresponsible actions by a few could mean all anglers being banned from fishing the pier. Leaving litter is one thing that really upsets owners and has lead to many piers and harbour walls being closed to anglers. Clearing up behind you, whether the litter is your own or not, will set a standard that hopefully others will copy. We can ill afford to lose any more access to fishing spots in this overcrowded country.

SOCIAL FISHING

Fishing from a pier is very different from standing alone on a remote beach, as there are always other anglers around to chat to. Many will have fished the pier before and it's always worth asking where the hot spots are, what's the best bait and time of the tide to fish. Occasionally through the year there are competitions on many of the piers — the Christmas ones are a particular favourite — and with everyone fishing in such close proximity it makes for a great atmosphere with plenty of laughs throughout the day. While many anglers enjoy the solitude and silence of angling alone, it can be great fun once in a while to enjoy some social fishing.

HOW MANY RODS?

Most piers make a charge for each rod, not each angler. Sometimes it works well to have two rods as one can be cast out for bottom fishing and then some more active fun can be had with a float on another rod. A rod for mackerel can be kept ready as a shoal may only pass by once in the day and it pays to be ready for them. Apart from the obvious fact that the

fresh fish make good eating, they are also a good
fresh bait. If the use of two rods is permitted it may
be an idea to have two identical sets of tackle, and
cast one a long way out and the other close to the
pier giving you a double option on finding the fish.

TROLLEYS

Some piers are extremely long and it can be useful
to have some sort of trolley or set of wheels to
help transport your tackle. With a tackle box, bait
bucket, drop net, rod, and weights, the walk along
a pier can be quite tough. Alternatively, fix some
small wheels to your tackle box like those used to
pull suitcases along at airports. Anything to make
the day easier will help your concentration on the
fishing better.

NO MESS

Leave the pier in a tidy condition when you leave.
Having to clean up after anglers is one good reason
local authorities can use to have fishing banned.
Don't take up too much room, with tackle strewn
about, as other anglers may come and fish next to
you and holidaymakers are prone to tripping over
odd bits of tackle left around. Try to get on with
the anglers around you and enjoy the experience.

PIERS, BREAKWATERS AND MARINAS

Here are a few of the top piers on our coastline
worth a visit:

Roker Pier

One of the longest piers for shore anglers is the
Roker pier at the mouth of the river Wear. It is
around a mile in length with a good depth of water
for a couple of hours each side of high tide. The
pier is safe to fish from as it has rails either side,
but is succeptable to bad weather when the local
council will close the gates to anglers. The pier is
well known for its catches of coalies, cod and
whiting. Top bait is peeler crab, but mussels,
lugworm, ragworm, mackerel and herring all catch
at various times through the year.

Ilfracombe Pier

The pier at Ilfracombe is not your traditional long
pier jutting out to sea, but more a walkway round
a rocky mark protruding into the Bristol Channel.
The fishing area is split into three areas with the
lowest section in the middle the most popular. Grip
leads are essential as the tide can be quite strong.
Winter fishing produces whiting, dogfish and pout
with some decent cod showing up each year; large
congers are regularly hooked through the summer
and autumn; small-eyed ray, plaice, red mullet,
bream, mackerel and garfish all show up at various
times during the year; grey mullet shoals arrive in
the summer and can be caught on bread flake by
the dedicated angler using light tackle. Other
species that have been landed from the pier
include trigger fish and blonde ray. For bait try any
worm bait, peeler crab, sand eel or mackerel.

Brighton Marina West Arm

The west arm at Brighton is a very convenient

platform to fish from and can produce some excellent catches, particularly bass. The arm is well policed, kept tidy and in good condition with regular patrols. Plenty of mackerel and garfish on the float through the summer with flatfish and bass on the bottom. Winter fishing is good for whiting, pout and codling.

Worthing

This West Sussex pier is a super venue for mullet, pollack and flounders in summer, and whiting, pout and codling in winter. The fishing is restricted to certain areas and only underarm casting is allowed, but there are plenty of fish within the close proximity of the pier. Other species such as dabs, smoothhound and plaice can be caught through the spring and summer months. Ragworm, lugworm, maddies and white rag catch most of the fish in the summer while lugworm tipped with mackerel or squid will catch plenty of whiting and pout in the winter months.

Weymouth Stone Pier

There are two piers at Weymouth. The shorter one is accessed by the Pavilion theatre and has some cover from the weather on it. The longer Stone pier can only be accessed from the Brewers Quay side of the river and stretches for over quarter of a mile, pointing out across Weymouth bay. This is a popular match venue with local clubs as there are always fish to catch. There are numerous small wrasse, pout, pollack and the odd coalie, close in to the sides which the local schools league target in their regular matches. Through the summer float fishing produces mackerel, garfish and pollack with whiting, pout and codling showing up in winter. The excellent Weymouth Angling Centre provides good quality fresh bait and plenty of advice to the visiting angler.

South Pier, Lowestoft

Although a fairly short pier, Lowestoft's south pier does have deep water round it. It's constructed of solid concrete with a handy sized wall all round that makes for safe fishing. At the shore end of the pier there are facilities for food and drink. The main target here are the codling and whiting that can be caught throughout the autumn and winter. In the summer the bass and eels make a show with a few flatfish such as dab, sole and flounder. Most popular bait is lugworm for the whiting and codling, and ragworm and fish baits come next as favourites. Lugworm tipped off with squid will often produce more fish than other baits.

Steetley Pier, Hartlepool

The pier supports two large pipes that run along each side creating a convenient safety barrier and rod support. It is a renowned cod mark that fishes best after a north easterly gale when the cod will come in close to pick up the shellfish washed out of the sand. At other times using shellfish as bait will catch flatfish. Bass are another feature at Steetley with fish over 10 lb having been landed, and whiting are prolific during the winter months. The best baits are lugworm, ragworm, razors and peeler crab. Tides can be strong, and leads from 5 oz to 10oz can be required at times and always use a strong leader so fish can be hauled up onto the pier as the pipes make the use of a drop net difficult.

South Parade Pier, Portsmouth
At less than 200 metres, the South Parade Pier at Portsmouth is one of the shorter ones. Fishing is carried out on the lower jetty at the far end of the pier. Safe railings, at a height that makes them ideal rod rests, surround the pier. There's float fishing through the summer for garfish, mackerel, pollack, pout and scad. Smoothhound and bass will be caught on peeler crab with prawns a good alternative. Casting from the right of the pier into clean ground will produce excellent results for plaice and smooth hound. Lugworm is the top bait with ragworm a close second. Cocktails of squid and rag will tempt the flatfish during the spring.

Holyhead Breakwater, Anglesey
This massive structure was made from local stone with a wall to the left and a wide flat stone walkway. It makes an ideal fishing platform and produces some big fish: most notably congers and bull huss. Big fish baits are needed for these species and fishing at night from the end by the lighthouse is the best time. Elsewhere on the breakwater there are plenty of species such as whiting, codling and dabs in winter and pollack, wrasse, coalfish, bass, dogfish and smooth hounds in summer. Several baits work well with lug tipped mackerel, mussels, peeler crab, fish baits and sand eels all producing fish at various times in the year.

Porthcawl, Wales

There are two piers, or breakwaters, protecting the entrance to the harbour at Porthcawl, with the lighthouse pier being the favoured fishing platform. Catches include rays, dogfish, whiting, flounders, dabs, pollack, pout, bass and smoothhound. There are always shoals of mackerel and garfish to be found in the summer when the piers become very busy. Care must be taken in rough seas as the waves can come over the outside wall, and lines must be removed for any boats entering the harbour as the entrance is so narrow. The best baits include lugworm, ragworm, peeler crab, mackerel and squid.

Mumbles Pier, Nr Swansea

The Mumbles pier is built on cast iron piles with the typical Victorian lattice steel work. It only protrudes about 200 metres out to sea but it is a favourite spot for sea anglers. It's got a convenient height railing all round that doubles as a rod rest, and there are several species of fish that can be caught here. The range of fish include mackerel, garfish, codling, whiting, bream, gurnard, bass, mullet, smoothhound and wrasse, with occasional catches of ray and triggerfish. All the regular baits will catch, such as lugworm, ragworm, peeler crab, sand eel, squid and mackerel.

The Barrage, Cardiff Bay

The massive investment into the Cardiff Harbour and surrounding area has eventually lead to anglers benefiting from a new mark to fish. The Barrage, built to protect the harbour, has only recently been opened up to anglers, who can fish from clearly defined areas marked by yellow lines and boxes on the promenade. It's worth trying all baits as the area can produce more or less anything; plenty of bass and some decent cod, dogfish, whiting and flatfish. Harbour authorities are fairly strict so take your litter home and make sure you get off the Barrage before closing time, otherwise this facility could be closed to anglers.

Penarth Pier
Not far from The Barrage is Penarth Pier. Another Victorian pier built with cast iron piles and diamond shaped metal work between. The pier is neat and tidy with the centre section reserved for anglers who have to keep to an area behind a broad white line. Visitors to the pier must keep out of this area for their own safety although there is no fishing through the summer months of June, July and August, when it's very busy with holidaymakers. Whiting, codling, bass, congers, sole, flounder, mullet, pout, mackerel, garfish, dogfish and ray can all be caught from this excellent pier that has toilets and a food kiosk to hand. Mackerel, squid, lugworm, ragworm and frozen sand eel are top baits at Penarth.

Folkestone Pier, Kent
The pier at Folkestone is a popular one as it offers plenty of room with fishing allowed all down one side, and it doesn't suffer from too much tidal flow. Lugworm is easy to obtain locally and it catches most fish the pier has to offer. In summer it boasts all the usual species such as pollack, pout, bass, eel, mackerel and a few plaice, while a good

run of whiting and codling can be expected in late autumn along with dabs and pout. The lugworm can be tipped off with fish bait for the whiting.

Dover Breakwater & Admiralty Pier

The famous cross channel port of Dover has two superb fishing marks for the shore angler. The breakwater has produced some amazing catches over the years but can only be accessed by boat. For a small fee anglers can be transported to the Breakwater at set times, but booking is advised as clubs block book it for some of their matches. The potential for fishing is enormous with specimen bass and large cod caught every year. In summer, shoals of big mullet can be targeted, along with bass, pollack, pout and flounder. Winter sees the arrival of vast shoals of whiting, pout and codling. Use bread for the mullet and lug, and crab for the cod, and try just about any other baits available as nobody knows what can turn up on this man-made breakwater so far offshore. Big tides can make fishing difficult so 8 oz to 10 oz grapnels may be necessary to hold bottom at times.

The Admiralty pier has space for several hundred anglers and regularly hosts big competitions. The fishing is similar to the Breakwater with some fairly strong tides. Lugworm, peeler crab, ragworm and fish baits are best for general fishing, or take bread and a bag for groundbait if going for mullet.

Southend Pier, Essex

The pier at Southend is famous for being the longest pleasure pier in the world. This gives a lot

of scope for sea anglers as there's plenty of room
for all. Some areas of the pier can't be fished, but
there are vast areas where it's permitted. In winter
there are plenty of whiting, codling, dab and the
ever-present pout to be caught. Best bait is
lugworm on it's own or tipped with squid or
mackerel. Summer sees a wide range of species
passing through including eel, flounder, mullet,
bass, garfish and mackerel, with peeler crab
considered the top bait.

Saltburn Pier, Cleveland
The recently refurbished Saltburn pier is one of the
few originally built in the area during Victorian
times that's still standing. Stretching over 250
metres out to sea, with fishing from both sides, it
gives good access to codling, whiting, bass and
flatfish. Local anglers fish with lugworm and
ragworm — sometimes tipped with fish bait. After a
gale, collect some shellfish off the beach and add
these to the worm baits. Long casting is not usually
needed on this pier.

Port Logan, West Scotland
This relatively short breakwater with a lighthouse
on the end is best fished in decent weather as
waves can push up onto the rocks — especially in a
north westerly. There are plenty of pollack,
codling, dogfish and wrasse to catch most of the
year with the chance of a conger as well. Baits
such as crab, lugworm and ragworm all catch fish
regularly, while it pays to try a spinner or artificial
eel for the pollack.

BOAT FISHING

Fishing from a boat gives the sea angler a chance to tackle some of the bigger fish found round our coastline, such as conger, tope, ling, blonde ray, bull huss, pollack and cod. There are also a host of other species that the boat angler can catch that rarely come within the range of the shore angler. Turbot, brill and large plaice that are found on the offshore banks are a much sought after target for boat anglers. If you own your own boat you have the freedom to fish the marks you want, and to move around in search of the different species that you don't have in a charter boat. On the flip side, you will be limited on the distance you travel due to the size of boat and weather conditions, and you won't have the skipper's experience of the tides and location of where the fish are. This can of course be learnt over a period of time.

➣ Boat fishing gives access to some of the larger fish in the sea.

CHARTER BOATS

Charter boat fishing is very popular with boats operating out of most ports in the UK. For those anglers who don't own their own boat or live near the sea it's an ideal way of getting afloat and catching some good fish. The modern day charter skipper will have a fast, stable boat, brimming with all the latest electronics and have the expertise to put you over the fish. It's a very sociable way of fishing as there will probably be several other anglers on board. There's no limit to how much fish you can take home with you, but most skippers encourage conservation and the return of any fish not wanted for eating. If there are fish you want to take back to eat the skipper will often clean it on the way back to port and provide a bag to take it home in.

☞ **Charter boat fishing is a very social way of fishing.**

Booking a boat

A charter boat trip needs to be planned and booked up in advance, especially during the times and tides when there are good catches to be made. Many of the top boats are booked up months in advance so allow plenty of time ahead to get what you want. There are lists of charter boats on several websites with details of availability and prices. First call the skipper and book a date; you will then have to send a deposit. If you don't turn up on the day this will be lost, but if the skipper has to cancel because of the weather he will offer you another date or return the deposit. Call the skipper the day before the planned trip to see if it's still on, and check what species are likely to be caught and which baits need to be purchased. Make sure you are in good time in the morning as the skipper may have organised the trip to get the best out of the tides.

☞ **Always check in with the skipper the day before the trip.**

Equipment

One of the biggest gripes charter skippers have is the amount of gear the anglers take on board. Large tackle boxes, weight buckets, cooler boxes and rod bags are all necessary, but if you are travelling with someone else try to share things like bait containers and weights. Take a couple of rods — one for around 12 to 15lb class and another of 20 to 30lb class — which will cover just about any type of fishing. Mackerel feathers are likely to be the first thing required for bait collection so have them handy. Suitable clothing is very important as it can be quite cold offshore even while on the beaches people are sunbathing. A lightweight waterproof is vital as a quick shower can leave you soaked, and the wind will chill anyone not protected. Thermal flotation suits are very popular for winter fishing as they keep the body warm, and in the event of an accident act as a life preserver.

🐟 **Remember it can be cold at sea even when the sun is out.**

Food and drink

Most charter skippers will make a cup of tea during the day — in fact many make several — but you shouldn't rely on it. Take a flask of tea or coffee and enough food for the trip with you as the trip could last at least eight hours. Try to pack a good mixture of sandwiches, fruit and chocolate bars, rather than the convenience foods like meat pies and sausage rolls. Even if you have a flask, a bottle of water is important especially during the summer months. If you want something hot while afloat you could take a cup-a-soup or a pot noodle, as the skipper can always provide some hot water for you. It's surprising how uplifting a bit of hot food can be on a winter trip after cod.

🐟 **Most skippers make a cup of tea but don't rely on it.**

Seasickness

One thing that can ruin a great day out in a charter boat is feeling seasick. There are several things that can help prevent it, one being a good breakfast, not too fatty, before the trip. Things like scrambled egg or grilled tomatoes on toast help to settle the stomach. Porridge is another good food for calming the system before a trip. Don't drink heavily the night before as this is almost certain to cause problems. Anyone who suspects they might feel queasy should take some form of travel sickness tablet; even if it isn't required it can give that extra bit of confidence to someone who might otherwise have suffered.

🐟 **Avoid drinking heavily the night before a charter boat trip.**

Bait

During the summer months the skipper will stop the boat before the fishing properly commences to collect mackerel for bait. Everyone will drop over a set of feathers and the bait is pooled for everyone to use later. Other times of the year the mackerel can't be relied on and some frozen bait should be taken. Even in summer it's well worth taking a box or two of squid, as there are many species that prefer it to mackerel. In winter when the likely target is cod it will be neccesary to take plenty of squid. This means taking at least a 5lb box each as big squid baits are best for big cod. In some areas where the fishing is inshore for codling a few packets of lugworm are a must. If the skipper has planned to do some specialised fishing, for example for smoothhound, tope, bream or bass, he will tell you before the trip so the correct bait can be ordered beforehand. Live sand eels are brilliant bait for bass, pollack and plaice, but need to be carefully looked after with an aerator in a bucket of seawater; peeler crabs are expensive but will often pick out the better fish; ragworm are available in most tackle shops and will catch a wide range of species.

🦐 **For winter cod fishing take plenty of squid.**

Protocol

With several anglers on the boat there are some things that can help make the trip a pleasure. Make sure the skipper has a clear passage round the boat as he will want to get round to net any good fish. Store spare rods away somewhere in the cabin or rod racks, keep tackle boxes out of the way and don't leave tackle with hooks laying around on the deck. If any bait is dropped on the deck wipe it up before anyone slips over. If your line gets tangled with another angler don't get mad, keep calm and sort it out. Nobody wants to lose fishing time but sometimes when the tide is turning or a fish is hooked it can get round another line. It can't be helped and is not generally anyone's fault so just deal with it. When an angler close to you hooks a large fish either move away to give them room to play the fish or even wind in your line. If tangles start to occur too often it needs the anglers near the cabin to put on a slightly bigger weight to prevent running downtide into the other lines. If you are in a position on the boat that allows you to cast it may be worth getting your tackle away from the rest of the lines to prevent tangles occurring.

🐟 **Keep the area near you clear so the skipper can get around with the landing net.**

DRIFT FISHING

Many charter boat trips are spent on the drift, particularly wrecking trips. The skipper will find a suitable wreck and drift back over it several times if the fish are there; he may have to move to another wreck if one isn't fishing well. You need to be ready, as the drifts may not last long if the tide is fairly strong. As the boat gets near the wreck the skipper will probably call out a warning so the lines can be wound off the bottom to avoid snagging. Listen out for instructions from the skipper and when he calls 'lines up' get your tackle up quickly as he may need to move the boat for another drift or to avoid another boat or crab pot marker.

🐟 **Listen carefully as the skipper will warn you as you approach the wreck.**

Flying collar

The best way to fish a wreck on the drift is with a fixed boom, called a 'flying collar', with a trace of around one to two metres for shad or longer for live sand eels, artificial sand eels or jelly worms. The lures are lowered to the bottom at the start of the drift and wound back up for 20 or 30 turns of the reel. The fish will follow the lure, grab it and head back down to the wreck. This will pull the rod over and pull line off the reel. As soon as this initial run has slowed you can start to pump the rod and wind in. Have the clutch set so the fish can dive again if it's a good one. Too many big fish have been lost because the clutch is wound up tight and the line breaks as the fish makes a dive for the bottom. The power of a coalfish or pollack on the first dive is amazing and they should be allowed to go, as you will break the line if you try to stop them.

☞ **Have the drag on the clutch set so the fish can easily take off line.**

At anchor

If your trip is an inshore trip where the boat will anchor a reef or particular patch of seabed, the tackle and tactics will be quite different from drifting a wreck; generally speaking it will mean bait fishing at anchor. Traces don't need to be so long and a running leger is often the best rig to use. Check with the skipper what fish are likely to be found in the area and adjust your tackle to suit. For rays, small conger and bull huss a fairly strong

trace of 60 lb—80 lb will be required. If the boat is
anchored into a wreck and there are big congers, a
trace of 150 lb may be neccesary. Much of the time
for general fishing of bream, pollack, codling and
other small fish a 30 lb trace is more than
adequate. Hook size is important as it should suit
the size of bait but not be too big for the fish. A
size 1 or 1/0 are a good choice to start with until
the species and size of fish in the area is
established.

🦀 **A good choice to start with on a new mark is
a size 1 or 1/0 hook.**

UPTIDE FISHING

In many areas where the water is fairly shallow
and fast-moving the skipper will suggest uptiding.
This means casting a grip lead at a 45% angle to the
front of the boat and allowing the weigh to get a
grip by feeding line out to create a bow in the line.
Tackle for this method of fishing is with a rod of
around 3 metres with a casting reel, either a
smallish multiplier or a large fixed spool. The tackle
is quite simple using a short boom, which can be a
fixed or running type of boom with a trace of about
a metre. This method is used in places like the
Thames estuary, the Mersey, the Humber and the
Bristol Channel, and proves very successful. Part of
the reason for its success is it guarantees the bait is
firmly fixed on the bottom where the fish can home
in on it using the scent trail.

🦞 **Allow enough line off the reel for the weight to grip.**

COSTS

A day out charter fishing will cost from £35 for inshore trips up to £55 per person for wrecking trips. This could be seen to increase in view of the way fuel costs are still rising. Add to this the cost of any tackle and bait required for the trip, fuel to drive to the venue and parking, and it can come to a considerable amount. This is why you need to pick your skipper carefully; no one minds paying out if they get good value for their money. This doesn't always mean catching lots of fish. If the skipper makes you welcome aboard, helps with advice, makes a cup of tea and tries hard all day to find the fish it can be a pleasant experience. Obviously when there are plenty of fish coming over the side it puts smile of everyone's face, but it can't happen every time. So ask other anglers who they recommend, read the magazines to see who catches good fish regularly and ring up a few and ask what they have been catching lately. This will all build a picture of the best skipper to go out with.

🦞 **A charter boat trip is good value for the money.**

BRAID OR NYLON

The question of which type of line to fill reels with is very much a matter of choice, although in recent years braid has become the favourite. It's easy to see why braid is so widely used. It's very strong, very thin and has no stretch — so let's look at these properties in more detail. Braid is very strong but not very good where abrasion is concerned. This is why a decent length of mono (nylon) leader should be used as it can take much more of the abrasive type of wear and tear. Braid is much thinner than a comparable breaking strain of mono. This reduced diameter allows less weight to be used in deep water and strong tides. As braid is non-stretch bites can be felt much easier, but being so direct can pull a hook free if correct clutch setting is not set or a soft enough rod is not used. Knots are more difficult to tie in braid as it has a Teflon like ability to slip when pulled tight. Use a spot of super glue on the knot just to make sure it stays tight; if mono is used as main line, bites will be a little more difficult to detect, but if a fast moving fish like a bass is hooked it is far more likely to be landed as the stretch in the line irons out any mistakes the angler makes in playing the fish.

🐟 **Less weight is needed with braid as it is much thinner than mono.**

HOOKS

Second in importance to the bait in any fishing must be the hook: as it's the first contact point the angler has with the fish. A hook must firstly be suitable for the size of bait being used. It must be very sharp and it should be strong enough to hold the species being targeted. This mention of targeting fish is important as most fish will be caught by design not by luck. You will be fishing in an area renowned for a particular species and your bait will be one to catch it. There will always be surprise catches, but generally you will catch what you set out for. Smaller hooks and baits catch more fish but they also attract small fish. To catch the better fish you may need to up the size of the bait and hook to ensure a quality fish is caught.

🐟 **Hooks should be sharp and suitable for the size of bait being used.**

OWNING A BOAT

FREEDOM

One of the last great unlicensed freedoms in the UK is to own your own boat. To be able to go out to marks you have found, or picked off an admiralty chart, and to catch your own fish gives a great sense of achievement. But with this freedom comes responsibility, especially if friends or family are likely to be on board. The boat should be seaworthy enough for the area of coastline being fished and the engine in good working order. There should be enough lifejackets for all on-board, and a VHF radio is a must in case help needs to be called. A mobile phone is useful but can't be relied upon the further out to sea you go. In a small open dinghy a set of oars are essential to help with launching, and if the engine should fail they become another means of propulsion. In bigger boats a small spare engine can be carried, and many a time this has saved experienced boat anglers the embarrassment of calling the lifeboat out.

🐟 **A mobile phone is useful for inshore fishing but the signal is lost just a few miles offshore.**

MOORING OR TRAILING

One aspect of boat fishing many people tend to forget when they visit a Boat Show or see a bargain boat for sale is where they are going to keep it. Here are a few things to take into consideration when thinking of keeping a boat at home and trailing it to the sea each time. Is the driveway big enough to keep a boat on a trailer — remembering that the trailer is a lot bigger than the boat itself? Is the car powerful enough to tow a large boat and is insurance cover available? The most important thing about trailing a boat is looking after the trailer; if it has been backed into the salt water on the previous launch the brakes can seize up with salt so regular attention with a grease gun is essential. The tyres are another vital item to be kept in tip-top condition for a long journey. A spare wheel with fully inflated tyre needs to be carried, as a puncture on a lonely stretch of road can be frustrating as well as expensive if help has to be called for. The alternative is to find a mooring for the boat; this could be a space in a compound or a floating berth. The floating berth is the ideal but charges in a marina even for a small boat are very expensive and often there is a long waiting list. Check out the availability and costs before purchasing your boat. A cheaper option is an open water berth where a small dinghy or tender will be needed to ferry you to and from the boat.

🐟 Buying a boat is easy — where to keep it can be a problem.

OUTBOARD MOTORS

Generally speaking boats less than 20 feet in length use outboard motors while larger boats are designed for inboard engines. Modern 4-stroke outboard motors are very quiet compared with 2-stroke engines, with much improved economic performance. Boat manufacturers have to state the maximum size outboard their boats are designed for, and it's important to keep to this advice as it may invalidate the insurance if a more powerful one is fitted. Outboards are simple to operate and make control of the boat very easy. The 4-stroke outboard needs very little maintenance with an oil check required every few weeks while the older 2-stroke outboard has to have oil mixed to the petrol each trip.

🐟 Using an outboard motor larger that the boat is designed for may invalidate the insurance.

INBOARD ENGINES

Larger boats have inboard engines as it allows much bigger engines to be fitted and they balance the boat better. Most inboards are diesel, and as they are inside the boat can be worked on while at sea if a problem arises.

SAFETY EQUIPMENT

It's important to have the correct safety equipment as conditions can change dramatically at sea and they need to be easily accessible. A lifejacket of some sort for all on-board is a must; in small dinghies it's advisable to wear them at all times. If a problem occurs you need to be able to let someone else know where you are and for this reason a VHF radio is crucial; a distress call on channel 16 will bring an immediate response from the local coastguard. Mobile phones are useful but lose the signal a few miles offshore. Other items that should be carried include spare fuel: running out of fuel is one of the most common problems that inexperienced boat anglers suffer from. Assisting another boat by towing them will also use extra fuel. Always have an anchor on the boat even if you don't intend to use it. In the event of a breakdown, putting the anchor down will stop the boat drifting away from the search area and make assistance easier. A compass, first aid kit and a torch are other essentials.

🐟 **Having a VHF radio on-board is crucial if help is required.**

ANCHORING

For bottom fishing the boat needs to be anchored, and to do this successfully a proper length of rope, chain and correct size of anchor is required. Firstly, the length of rope should be at least three times the depth of water; for example in 20 metres of water use 60 metres of rope. This is so the angle to the anchor forces it into the bottom and won't be bounced out as the boat goes up and down on the waves. To doubly ensure the anchor stays in the bottom a length of chain is fixed between the anchor and rope; as a rough guide the chain should be one and a half times the length of the boat. A 6-metre boat would need 9 metres of chain. The type of anchor can be a matter of choice with the three main types being the Fisherman's, the Plough and the Danforth. The Fisherman's is good in mixed broken ground while the other two are good in sandy and muddy areas. For very rough or rocky areas a grapnel is the best bet as it can be pulled free by sustained pressure on the bendable spines.

☞ **In very rocky areas use a grapnel that can be pulled free.**

RETRIEVING THE ANCHOR

One of the danger points while fishing from small boats is retrieving the anchor. Most boat anglers use an Alderney ring with a large buoy attached. This method can be operated from the cockpit of the boat with no need to clamber on the bow as used to be the way. The anchor rope runs through the Alderney ring and when the boat is driven forward at 45% from the line of the anchor the buoy slides back down the rope and the water pressure lifts the anchor. With forward motion the ring continues down the chain to the anchor and the chain then acts as a counter balance preventing the anchor from sliding back to the bottom again. Now it's just a matter of feeding the rope back into the boat as the anchor is suspended under below the buoy. The practice of clambering up on the bow of a small boat, tossing about in a bumpy sea, trying to pull up the anchor is a sure way to have an accident. By using the Alderney ring method means it's worked safely from the cockpit of the boat. One thing to note is make sure the anchor is tied to the bow and never fix the rope to the stern of the boat: this is how boats are pulled under and sunk.

🐟 **When using the Alderney ring a careful watch must be kept to see the anchor rope doesn't get anywhere near the outboard motor.**

PLANNING YOUR TRIP

To get the very best of a day afloat some forward planning is essential. The weather forecast is the first thing to consider; anything over a force 4 wind, unless it's blowing offshore, would not be suitable for a boat under 5 metres long. The tides are very important in helping decide where you will be fishing and what species are likely to be there. On spring tides make sure you have enough weights for the area you will be fishing and allow plenty of anchor rope out to ensure it will grip in the strong current. Bait will have to be ordered if such things as lugworm, ragworm, live sand eel or peeler crab are needed; try to keep bait cool right up to when you begin to start using it as having top quality bait is the one thing that will influence the success of a days fishing. Make up several suitable rigs before the trip so if any are lost on the bottom or get

tangled a replacement is ready; keep everything
tidy and easy to find in your tackle box. A shoal of
fish may come on the feed or be spotted and if
suitable tackle can't be found quickly the chance
of catching them could be lost.

🐟 Always let someone know the area you intend
fishing and your expected time of return.

TACKLE FOR DINGHY FISHING

Apart from areas where the tides are very strong
and the fish very large, a light to medium set of
tackle will land just about anything likely to be
caught. Rods should be between 7 ft and 10 ft in
length and rated at between 12 lb and 20 lb.
Generally the main line can be anything from 12 lb
to 20 lb if using mono (nylon) but a heavier leader
of around 30 lb is advisable especially if casting
uptide or while fishing in rough ground. When using
braid it's advisable to go for slightly heavier main
line such a 30 to 40 lb as it's far thinner than mono
but more susceptible to abrasion. Because of this a
mono leader of around 6 metres is required for the
braid. Reels can be medium sized multipliers or
salt water fixed spools. When braid is used as the
main line it requires less weight to hold bottom
due to the thin profile of the line. Every bite is
magnified due to the non-stretch property of braid
and care must be taken not to strike too early.

🐟 When using braid as main line always use a
mono leader to take the abrasion of the sand,
gravel or rocks on the bottom.

BAIT

Good quality live bait will always be best and thought must be taken in choosing which to use on a dinghy trip: ragworm and lugworm will be best in a mainly sandy bottom where species such as plaice, dabs, whiting, codling and gurnard will be caught. Peeler crabs are expensive but they will pick out different species such as ray, cod and smoothhound. Mackerel, squid, herring and cuttlefish are used in deeper water or over a rough bottom where the bigger fish like huss, bass and conger can be found. It's important to keep the bait in tip-top condition and is best placed in a cool box with a couple of ice blocks. Prawns and shrimps are often overlooked as bait but they are attractive to several species including bass and smooth hound.

🐟 **A cool box will help keep bait in tip-top condition.**

FISHING AT ANCHOR

It seems an obvious thing to say, but to get the best out of anchor fishing you need an anchor that works. There's nothing more frustrating than getting settled on a good fishing ground and having the anchor slip. By following all the guidance regarding length of rope and chain in the paragraph on 'Anchoring' (page 71) it will ensure the boat stays put.

DOWN TIDE

Fishing down tide, out the back of the boat, generally works best with a running leger and a flowing trace; this allows the bait to work naturally in the tide. It takes a while to get the first bites, as a scent trail builds up, but can be added to by using a rubby-dubby or groundbait. Any fish bait or leftover bait can be cut up and crushed before letting down in a weighted bag or in a specially made bait dropper. This brings the fish on the feed and can hold them in the area of the baits. Most fish can be caught down tide using traces of between one or two metres but it can be worth trying longer ones if bites are slow. For ray fishing it's generally best to keep the trace fairly short, as they prefer to smother their prey on the bottom. Make sure to give bites time to develop before striking; in fact it's usually best not to strike but to wind up the slack line until the weight of the fish is felt then lean back into it as you start to wind to set the hook.

🐟 It can take a while before the first bites are felt, as a scent trail needs to develop.

UPTIDING

In shallow areas where there is a good tide run the most successful method is uptide casting; this is not as complicated as it sounds. All it involves is putting a grapnel or breakaway lead on and casting towards the front of the boat at a 45% angle from the anchor. Let out enough line for the weight to hit bottom then allow several metres more to create a bow in the line. Put the rod in a holder or on the transom and watch for bites. A decent fish will pick up the bait and pull the weight out causing the rod to straighten up. The rod should then be picked up quickly and the slack line wound in until the weight of the fish is felt, and pumped back to the waiting landing net. When casting, always call out a warning such as "casting" to warn others on the boat to be aware. Surprisingly few accidents happen while uptide casting, even on quite crowded boats. As a safety precaution hang the baited hook on one of the grapnel wires before casting and the hook will come free as the weight hits the water.

🐟 **Allow enough line out for the weight to grip and to create a bow in the line.**

DRIFT FISHING

Many boat anglers never drop an anchor as they like to drift for their fish. This method works best where the tides are less demanding or when fishing wrecks out deep and over inshore reefs. Tackle is quite different with a paternoster rig proving best for fish such as ling, wrasse, bream and whiting. This is a rig with fixed hooks above the weight and baited with ragworm, squid or mackerel strip. Baited Hokkai lures are very popular and catch a wide variety of fish. Various artificial lures can be used on a long trace for fish such as bass, cod and pollack over the wrecks and reefs. These are lowered to the bottom and slowly retrieved by winding up to 35 turns on the reel. Count the number of turns until the lure is taken, so next drop down you can wind back to that depth the fish are feeding.

🐟 **When using artificial lures wind up as much as 35 turns to find the fish.**

COMPETITION FISHING

One of the quickest ways to learn about boat fishing is to take part in a charter boat competition where other anglers will be aboard. Don't be shy and ask questions of what methods and tackle they are using. Everyone can learn from others and shared knowledge helps the general standard of angling to improve. The skipper of a charter boat will also be able to give advice on species, bait and which tackle to try. Watch the other anglers, especially the ones catching the most fish, as they will probably have slightly different tackle and tactics that are worth noting and putting to practice next time you go fishing. Top anglers are the ones who have plenty of tackle ready and easy to get at, as well as having a well-organised tackle box. By copying their methods you will improve your fishing and hopefully become a better angler. Many people are put off competitions as they feel it will be too cut-throat and they will look silly, but this is not the case. There's a definite camaraderie amongst all boat anglers and someone will always be willing to help a newcomer — it just needs you to ask.

🐟 **Watching other more experienced anglers is the quickest way to learn.**

ANGLING CLUBS

If you don't like the idea of fishing in competitions, then joining a club is another way to find out more about the sport; as most club members are thrilled to talk about where the fish are and how to catch them. Shared information is the way we learn about life, and the same applies in the fishing world. Having a place where other anglers gather and talk about fishing, such as in a clubhouse, is where valuable local information can be picked up. If you catch any good fish they can be weighed in officially at the club and may even win you a trophy at the end of the year.

🐟 **By joining a club you get to meet other like minded anglers.**

KAYAK FISHING

Without doubt one of the biggest crazes to hit boat fishing over the past five years is the use of kayaks. These unsinkable, lightweight and inexpensive craft have allowed a whole new range of people to come into the sport — in particular the young and adventurous among us. There are several reasons for the uptake of this somewhat precarious sport. There's the fact more or less anyone can afford a kayak, they are light enough for a single person to launch on their own just about anywhere and can be transported easily on top of a car. They allow anglers to fish inshore marks in just a few feet of water where other boats can't get and they are virtually silent so fish can be approached without scaring them off. In sheltered waters of estuaries and bays protected from the wind they really come into their own.

🐟 **Kayak fishing is exciting but potentially dangerous and due care must be taken.**

SIT ON TOP

The modern kayak being used for sea fishing is referred to as a SOT Kayak. This stands for 'sit on top' rather than sitting inside the craft as with a canoe. The whole thing is a sealed unit that means it's unsinkable but anyone taking up the sport would benefit from being able to swim; in fact it's recommended that you don't take up fishing from a kayak unless you can swim. They are often equipped with a sonar fish finder, have storage compartments accessed through waterproof hatches and have a waterproof tackle box strapped behind the seat. With a couple of rod rests, a well-equipped kayak angler can fish in several ways: getting in close to rocks and inshore wrecks or obstructions to cast a lure for bass and pollack. Using the rod rests they can troll lures for bass, plus using lures and spinners and with a small anchor, they can bottom fish in areas where the tide is not too strong. There is even a kayak that can be paddled with the feet making it 'hands free', very handy for someone with a fishing rod in their hands.

🐟 **Kayak fishing can get you into marks other boats can't.**

SAFETY

The one aspect that must be stated is the safety angle. Even in expert hands a kayak angler should take precautions to have everything strapped down and be wearing a life jacket, and a dry suit to keep the wind off and to keep you warm in the event of going in the water. The chance of turning over is not great but always possible. Rather like a motorbike on the roads, a kayak on the sea is at the mercy of other irresponsible boat users who speed past too close; the wash from another boat is probably the biggest hazard a kayak angler faces. In particular the paddles should be fixed to the craft by a paddle leash so there's no chance of losing the only means of propulsion. If the kayak did turn over they can be easily be flipped back the right way and then it's a matter of pulling your torso back on board before sliding on one leg at a time to stabilise the craft and resuming the sitting position.

🖎 **Paddles should be attached to the boat at all times.**

CHOOSING A KAYAK

If possible talk to other owners before you dip your toe in the market. Their experiences may help you to choose the right sort of kayak. As a rule of thumb a long narrow one will go faster than a shorter, wider one, but the greater width will give more stability. It will mean taking a bit longer to get to the fishing grounds as they are a little harder to paddle.

🐟 Generally the wider the kayak the more stable it is.

PAIR UP

To start with never go alone on your first few trips at least. Go with someone who knows the ropes and can keep a watch on your progress. There's nothing so lonely as tipping over when you are all alone, especially if it's one of your first trips. In fact a good suggestion is not to take fishing gear with you on the first trip but use it to familiarise yourself with the way the kayak handles in broken water and in the waves or swell found at sea. Better still stick to sheltered inland water, a lake or harbour until the art of manoeuvring a kayak has become familiar.

🐟 For safety always team up with someone.

PADDLES

As the paddle is your main means of propulsion it is vital it's not dropped over the side and lost. This means using a paddle leash that fixes it to the craft. The size of paddle is down to the individual but they are usually between 2m and 2.40m in length. The length of your arms and whether you are slim or well built will all have a bearing on the size of paddles to suit you.

🐟 Chose a paddle to suit your arm length.

ELECTRONICS

It seems daft fixing an echo sounder and a VHF radio to such a small vessel but both will be very helpful. The sounder will of course show the bottom contour, allowing you to pick out likely fish holding areas while the VHF radio can be used to keep in touch with your friends or be used in an emergency. These need to be waterproof, as they will, one way or another, get a soaking. If a mobile phone is carried it should be safely encased in a waterproof bag as seawater and mobile phones are not good together.

🐟 **Keep mobile phones in a waterproof bag.**

HOT SPOTS

Here are some boat fishing marks to try in the UK with charter boats available:

🐟 **Owners of small boats and kayaks should choose areas where there is sufficient shelter for them to get afloat safely.**

Weymouth, Dorset

This is the premier fishing spot in the country as it has super fishing and plenty of charter boats with a very professional bunch of skippers. Portland Bill gives shelter from the southwest so very few trips are cancelled which is another consideration when booking a trip. Summer fishing is best with pollack, cod and congers on the wrecks, bass, bream, ray and bull huss on the banks, while inshore there are wrasse, pollack, triggerfish, bream and the ever present dogfish to be caught. The ray fishing can be excellent with blonde, undulate, small-eyed, thornback and spotted ray all caught on a regular basis. On the famous Shambles bank there's always a chance of a turbot, brill or plaice.

Whitby, Yorkshire
The premier northern port is without a doubt Whitby with a large fleet of charter boats working throughout the year. Cod and ling are the main target species and large catches can be made over the inshore wrecks with some quality specimens taken on most trips. Generally fishing is done on the drift with baited lures taking most of the fish. Recently more anglers have been using shads as an alternative to the baited rigs and have had great success with cod and some decent ling. The charter skippers association run a big month-long competition every summer with the largest fish caught during the period winning a big cash prize. Anglers fishing the inshore marks from their own boats will find that apart from the cod and ling there are a surprising number of other species to be caught including dabs, flounders, whiting and bass.

Poole, Dorset
The second biggest natural harbour in the world has a big fleet of charter boats and some excellent fishing. Inshore there are loads of bream, wrasse and triggerfish in late summer, while the wrecks produce big catches of cod and pollack. The undulating sand banks a few miles offshore are the home to smooth hound, ray and tope. Bass are a big feature in the catches off Poole through the

summer and in the winter the port is renowned for its large cod. In the extensive and sheltered waters of the harbour some terrific flounders to 4 lb can be caught during the winter months.

Plymouth, Devon

The reefs and wrecks round the Eddystone lighthouse are world famous for their catches of bass, pollack, ling and conger eels. Joyce Yallop's 500lb record mako shark was taken from this area and numerous other records have been set from the port. Many foreign anglers come to Plymouth every year to fish for conger eels as they have nothing like the quality and size of the fish the Devon port can boast. Many fish over 100 lbs have been recorded over the past decade and more are still being boated, although they are much more likely to be released nowadays. The pollack fishing is superb with many double figure fish, and in the early part of the year a few 20 lb specimens are regularly caught. Bass fishing round the Eddystone light using live sand eel is another feature of this legendary mark. There are plenty of charter boats to choose from but make sure you book a wreck or reef trip as costs are different and the type of tackle will need to be suitable.

Minehead, Somerset

The dirty waters of the Bristol Channel are a haven for many species of fish, and Minehead is an ideal port to get you out to them. With half a dozen charter boats and fishing within half-an-hours drive of the harbour it's an excellent venue. Inshore there are big smooth hound and several species of ray while offshore, in the middle of the channel, some large congers, tope and bull huss are likely. Packs of spurdog can turn up over the rough ground at any time while the winter cod fishing can be brilliant. Uptiding is the usual method for the cod and this also picks up congers right up to the end of the year in the channel.

Alderney, Channel Islands

Everyone should have at least one trip to the Channel Islands to fish Alderney. The fishing on the banks can be spectacular with some superb turbot and brill fishing on the drift. Bass fishing is probably the best in the whole of the UK and the tope fishing can leave you with aching arms. Several south coast charter skippers take regular parties to Alderney, usually a three-day trip with two nights away. This involves fishing in mid-channel on the way over, a full day fishing the banks and more fishing on the third day before returning port.

Fleetwood, Lancashire

Most opportunities for boat fishing in the northwest favour trailer boats but there is a charter boat at Fleetwood for those who don't own a boat. The fishing in the area can be really good with a wide range of species including tope, ray, bass, smooth hound, plaice, whiting, cod and some weighty bull huss turn up from time to time. Uptiding is the best method as the sea is fairly shallow and the current can run strongly on the spring tides. Grapnel leads from 6oz to 10oz are needed to keep the bait fixed on the bottom. Black lugworm are top bait for the plaice and tipped with squid will take whiting and codling. For the smooth hound and bass use peeler crab or other shellfish such as razors and mussel.

Lymington, Hampshire

Isle of Wight boats make Lymington their pick-up point and they then head out to the fishing grounds south of the famous Needles on the western end of the island. The area is renowned for big winter cod but at other times there is good bass fishing using float fished live baits such as mackerel, sand eel and pout. On the deeper banks large blonde ray, smooth hound, conger, pollack and bream are caught on a regular basis

Littlehampton, West Sussex

If you enjoy fishing for the hard fighting black bream then head for Littlehampton as the Kingmere rocks hold massive shoals of them each year, from late March through most of the year. In mid-summer there is a good run of quality bass and smooth hound while winter fishing sees plenty of big cod and hoards of whiting being caught. The regeneration of the waterfront has given the charter fleet better access and moorings near the town centre means anglers are again enjoying the benefits of this West Sussex port.

Brighton Marina, East Sussex

The Sussex port of Brighton has a good number of full time charter boats fishing the wrecks in mid channel. They take big catches of pollack and cod drifting the wrecks, and those that anchor down have terrific sport with some large congers. Fishing the ground at anchor there are black bream, ray and smooth hound through the summer while through the autumn and winter the whiting become prolific with a decent run of cod most years. Free parking is available close to the boats in the multi storey car park and a tackle and bait shop is right next to where the boats launch.

Amble, Northumberland

One of the gems of the north east is Amble: a very much under-rated port that produces some excellent fishing from the inshore marks. Fishing is mainly on the drift with jigging rigs with some sort of baited lure catching most of the fish. Leadheads, jellyworms and pirks will all catch pollack, cod, wrasse, coalfish and ling, especially when baited with lug, mackerel or as some locals do, cooked prawns! Gilling with a flying collar and a jellyworm on a long trace will pick out the better pollack. At anchor there are some good flatfish to be had including flounders, plaice, dabs and turbot.

River Mersey, Cheshire

It may sound crazy but fishing in the river Mersey close to the Liver building produces some of the best cod fishing in the country. With authorities working to keep our rivers clean, the sea fish have moved steadily further uptide so the sheltered waters of the Mersey have flourished. Charter boats can be booked at the new marina and although you may only travel a short distance the fishing can be impressive. Tides can be strong so uptiding with grapnel leads is the way to tackle up. A short trace with several lugworm on a 4/0 pennel rig is a sure way of catching the numerous codling. Generally the fish are not large with a double figure fish considered a good one for the area, but sport can be fast and furious. During the cod season, apart from lugworm, take squid and peeler crab if available. Through the summer when the bass, conger ray, smooth hound and various flatfish are in the river, ragworm and mackerel will be required.

Barry, south Wales
The south Wales port of Barry has access to some brilliant fishing in the Bristol Channel. The best method for the strong tides is to uptide with grapnel weights of 5oz to 10oz. Fishing with mackerel strip or peeler crab will catch a mixture of ray, smoothhound, tope, conger and huss with cod added to the mix in the winter. There are several species of ray during the summer and a good run of bass as well. Some of the boats will have a go for blue shark in late summer if the anglers request it.

Holyhead, Anglesey
The fishing in the Irish sea can be classed as all year round with plenty of species to try for from the wide variety of fishing grounds. The Welsh record for tope was caught from the port and with smoothhound to over 20lb always likely there's a great opportunity for some true sport fishing on light tackle. Not many trips are cancelled from Holyhead as there's plenty of shelter from most wind directions. The three main types of fishing you will need to be prepared for are: general bottom fishing over rough ground for conger, ray,

bull huss and smooth hound; inshore fishing for dabs, wrasse, whiting and pollack or wreck fishing for conger, cod, ling and pollack. Baited feathers, hokkai, shads and shrimp rigs can reap rewards at times for a greater mixture of species. All the usual bait such as mackerel, squid, ragworm, peeler crab and sand eels catch most fish while a cocktail mixture featuring a couple of the above can increase catches for some species.

Langstone Harbour, Hampshire

The charter boats out of Langstone can pick up anglers at Hayling Island on the east side of the entrance or at Southsea on the west. The boats have a super choice of areas to fish with Selsey Bill to the east and its superb smooth hound and tope grounds, or the area to the south of the Nab Tower with ray, bull huss and bass. If the wind is westerly they also have the shelter of the Isle of Wight where there is more good fishing spots for the small species such as bream and plaice. Big cod feature throughout the winter with plenty of whiting and spurdog to top up the catches.

LURE
FISHING

LURE FISHING

Catching fish in the sea without the use of bait is not new; feathers and spinners have long been an established way to catch certain species of fish. In recent years sea anglers have travelled abroad extensively, and brought back a wider range of lures they've seen working, to try them out for many of the UK species. Results have been surprising as most of them work to a greater or lesser degree, often dependent on the water clarity and the amount of time spent trying them out. Here are the most commonly used lures, how to fish with them and what you are likely to catch.

FEATHERS

The use of feathers to catch fish goes back hundreds of years to when it was a cheap and available option. Even today a set of small coloured feathers can be used to catch mackerel and pollack while a set of large white feathers on bigger hooks will catch cod. Generally the use of feathers has been taken over by new materials that are just as effective but more lasting such as silver foil, fish skin and various plastics.

SILVER SHRIMP

These are a very effective lure for several species including mackerel, garfish, scad, bass and codling. Made from silver foil, woven into a tube and secured with red whipping or a small piece of red tubing, they only need to be lowered to the bottom and jigged up and down. They can be baited to catch pout and bream in summer while in winter can make big catches of whiting. This was once thought of as an excellent bass lure particularly for the shoaling school bass.

SABIKI LURES

Although the trade name for one manufacturer, Sabiki has become the common name for any lure that has tiny hooks and generally used for bait collecting. Some of these lures are made with tiny size 12 hooks; these are used for catching sand eels, but suffer when a shoal of large mackerel show up, as they will smash the lures up. The pink Sabiki with size six hooks has become popular for small pollack and will even catch herring if there are some around. When using Sabiki's for launce put a shiny lure or pirk on the bottom instead of a lead weight as this will attract the fish to the lures. Don't jerk the rig up and down too sharply as this will result in lots of foul hooked sand eels and damage them in the process. Keep any damaged eels out of the main live bait tank as their blood can pollute the water and may kill off the rest.

HOKKAI LURES

When Hokkai lures first appeared in the tackle shops they quickly became all the rage. With a combination of feather, silver thread and a luminous plastic head, they made a very attractive and effective lure. It was amazing how many fish would seem to jump on them. Anglers still talk in amazement of what they, or other anglers, have landed on them: cod, bass, pout, pollack, bream, gurnard, garfish and whiting have all been taken in large numbers on the hokkai lures. The first batch of Hokkai's was made with size one hooks but they are now available in sizes up to 6/0 specifically for cod.

MINI SHRIMPS

Other manufacturers soon spotted the success of the Hokkai lures and it wasn't long before they had strong competition in the form of shrimp lures and mini shrimps. In effect these are smaller versions of the Hokkai and can be targeted at the smaller species of fish. They are a great bait catcher for mackerel, sand eel, pout or poor cod but have been put to good use by match anglers who just love to catch as many fish as possible when size really doesn't matter. Baited with ragworm, they catch several species of wrasse while a little strip of squid or mackerel will catch bream and gurnard and many other small species.

SPINNERS

Small spinners cast from the shore will catch mackerel, garfish, bass, scad and pollack. It's a fun way of fishing and keeps the cost down, as no bait is required. From rocky marks where there are weed and kelp beds a spinner wound fairly quickly, to keep it near the surface, will pick up pollack and sometimes a small bass. A light rod with a small fixed spool is all that's needed and using

braid instead of mono will give more control and
bite detection. Some charter boats in the West
Country still troll several spinners behind the boat
on the way to the fishing grounds picking up
enough mackerel for a days fishing.

ARTIFICIAL SAND EELS

Live sand eels were always the top way to catch
big pollack over the wrecks and reefs of the West
Country. When the supply of sand eels became a
problem Alex Ingram from Mevagissy invented an
artificial one that proved to be a winner. The Red
Gill has caught an amazing amount of fish over the
years and other manufacturers such as Eddystone
and Delta now make similar products that are also
excellent fish catchers.

The method used with these lures is to drift over
the marks using a flying collar and a long flowing
trace. Fish that will readily take these artificial
sand eels are garfish, mackerel, pollack, cod and
bass. Every now and then other species are caught
on them such as ling and John Dory. On tide races
and turbulent water big catches of bass have been
made with these lures that continue to be very
popular today.

JELLY WORMS

The jelly worm was first seen in the USA where
they were used to catch largemouth bass in the
lakes but it wasn't long before they proved
themselves in our seas. The best use for a jelly

worm is during the slacker tides as the tails need very little current to make them work. They will also catch more of the smaller species such as pout and even black bream on occasions. They are cheap to buy but don't last as long as the originals as the soft jelly can be easily bitten or chewed off. The black fire tail with a red or yellow tail has proved to be the most popular and effective, particularly for pollack, while the orange one seems to pick out the cod.

PIRKS

Who would have believed that treble hook on a lump of chrome pulled up and down near the seabed would catch fish? The Norwegians did, and they found in their cod-rich waters it was the quickest and most effective way to catch them. Now pirks are used widely throughout our waters although in recent years they have been superseded by the use of shads. Pirks don't need to be heavy, as the Swedish have shown with their skill of catching fish with lightweight pirks. Scottish anglers were quick to cotton on to this method and will cast a light pirk uptide as the boat drifts over the fish and work it back to the boat; what this does is keep the pirk working upright. If the pirk is just dropped to the bottom it works at a greater angle as the boat drifts away and becomes less effective. Pirking can be an expensive way to fish, as the treble hook often snags the wreck or reef, but on its day can make big catches. A good way to cut down on losses is to replace the treble hook with a single circle hook, as this will not snag the bottom but still catches fish.

LEAD HEADS

One way to prevent expensive losses when fishing on the drift is to use a lead head. This is in effect a weight with a fixed hook that is pointed up so it doesn't catch in the bottom. A jelly worm is slipped onto the hook shank and can be changed if it gets damaged. There are two ways to fish a lead head: one is by using a large one that will get to the bottom quickly and work it by lifting and dropping the rod tip to feel the weight hit the bottom. Cod are inquisitive and will come to the sound of the weight hitting the bottom then grab at the lure. The other way is to use a lighter lead head on a short trace of about a metre fixed to a boom with a suitable weight on. This is lowered to the bottom and bounced along the bottom so the lead head looks like it is a small fish diving for cover.

SHADS

Probably one of the biggest changes to lure fishing in recent years is the switch over to shads for catching cod, pollack and bass. When professional bass anglers use a lure then it's time to take note and they have gone for shads in a big way. They should be fished on the drift off a fixed boom with a trace of one to two metres. They need a good tide run to work best and they don't need to be bounced up and down on the bottom but just held steady. The stubby tail of the shad works well in the tide and the rampaging bass will chase and grab it with relish.

SIDEWINDERS

Following the success of the shads a new design
with a slightly slimmer and longer body has come
on to the market called a Sidewinder. These have
proved to be really effective for pollack, bass and
cod. Top colours have been the pearl, the mackerel
imitation and the latest craze for a red and yellow
one called 'rhubarb and custard'. Like shads the
design of the paddle tail makes them very effective
when worked near the bottom or slowly wound up
on a one to two metre trace.

MUPPETS

The use of an artificial squid, or 'muppet' as it's
known, can improve catches of several species.
Used a couple of feet above a pirk they will catch
cod, ling or pollack and by adding a strip of fish
bait it will make them even more attractive to
some species. Muppets can be used on flowing
traces where they should be slipped on the line
before the hook is added. To keep the muppet
above the bait, slip a few beads on before tying on
the hook, these act like a stop on top of the hook
keeping the bait exposed and the hook point free
from getting stuck in the muppet. They then slip
down to just above the bait and seem to draw fish
such as ling, bull huss and even congers to the bait.
For winter cod, a large muppet above a multi squid
bait catches some very big cod each year.

POPPERS

Fishing with surface poppers for bass is probably one of the most exciting methods of sea fishing. Poppers are a floating fish shaped lure with one or two treble hooks attached and a stubby concave nose. Using a light spinning rod and a fixed spool reel, the lure is cast over or near weed beds and then wound back in. By giving the rod a little jerk every now and then the flattened nose causes the lure to pop and jump in a frantic way. Bass see this as a fish in distress and attack it boldly. To see a big bass following the lure or surging up from beneath it is a heart stopping moment. This method can be carried out from a rocky shoreline or in dinghy or kayak where bigger boats can't get.

SALT-WATER FLY

The art of fly fishing for sea fish in the UK has taken off in recent years in a big way. While on holiday abroad, sea anglers have seen how effective fly fishing is for bonefish and other exotic species — even big game fish such as sailfish and marlin. This has lead to many anglers trying it in our waters for bass and pollack in particular. In late summer when bass can be seen close in chasing mackerel and white bait, is the best time to try it. From rocky marks fly fishing will catch pollack, especially during the evening and towards dusk. Tackle for both these species can be the same as used for trout fishing in the lakes. Some experimentation is needed to find the best fly for the different species.

BAITS

It doesn't matter whether you have a cheap second hand rod and reel or the latest equipment costing a small fortune, it's the quality and presentation of the bait that catches fish. It can't be emphasized enough that a few extra hours collecting bait, or a few extra pounds spent on buying the best bait, will catch you more fish that any other item in your fishing tackle. A sharp hook will help and fishing a productive mark an advantage, but if the baits no good, you won't catch fish. Buying the best you can or digging it yourself, then looking after it properly, will bring you the most success. Keeping bait cool, aerated if needed and getting it to the beach or boat in tip-top condition will be the biggest factor in your success as an angler. Here is a list of baits that regularly catch fish around our coast, in the boats and from the shore.

RAGWORM

Ragworm or king ragworm as they are known in some areas are probably the most widely used bait, and readily available from tackle shops. They are fairly easy to keep in peat, sand or vermiculite as long as they are kept cool. They are a large worm that is sometimes between 6 and 8 inches long. The big ones can be cut into sections for smaller fish or used whole for big bass, pollack, plaice, ray and smooth hound. The smaller worms will be readily taken by nearly all fish, making them an ideal bait for the holiday angler. It's not too expensive, clean to use and effective for a number of species. Off the rocks they can be used under a float for wrasse and pollack; in winter they will catch flounders in estuaries and harbours; while offshore they will catch whiting if used as a cocktail, tipping off a fish bait. The biggest drawback with ragworm is they don't freeze down. Any worm left over from a days fishing needs to be wrapped in clean dry newspaper and kept cool. Even so they will only last a day or two.

LUGWORM

Lugworm is another universal bait — except strangely in the South West of England where its use is very limited. Anywhere in the South East, East Anglia, North West and the North East it's probably the first choice, especially for shore anglers. There are more than one type of lugworm with the three main types being black lug, yellow tails and blow lug.

BLACK LUG

Blacks are the biggest of the lugworm family and are normally sold wrapped in newspaper. They are firm bait that can be cast a long way and are especially effective for cod. Black lugworm can be dug or pumped from sandy beaches but burrow quite deep and it takes a bit of practice to learn how to get them. They are also a great bait to use with another bait as a cocktail. When used in conjunction with squid or cuttlefish they can increase the range of fish they will catch. Thread one or more black lug up the line and tip off with a long thin strip of squid. This will still catch cod and whiting in winter, and during the summer months will catch plenty of black bream and flatfish. Black lug wrapped in newspaper and kept in the fridge will keep fresh for several days. They will also freeze down well so can be stockpiled for the winter when available.

YELLOWTAILS

A worm that is similar but a bit smaller than the black lug is the yellowtail. These are often sold live and are excellent bait. They do stain the fingers yellow but the juices from this type of worm are very attractive to most fish. Both the black lug and yellow tails will freeze down successfully. Yellowtails will keep for a few days in the fridge if put in a shallow tray with a little seawater. One tip for transporting them is to have a clean supply of seawater in the fridge to put them in for the journey to the sea. This water is then the same temperature as the water they had been kept in so they won't be traumatised by a dramatic temperature change.

BLOW LUG

Blow lug used to be dug extensively in this country and still can be in some spots, but are nowadays more likely to have been imported from Holland. They are small worms that are supplied live and are not suitable for freezing. Much cleaner to use than yellowtails but still have plenty of juice in them. They will soon lose their flavour in a strong tide and need re-baiting regularly. Blow lug casts can be seen well away from the low tide mark and are dug with a fork. Look for the worm in the second spit of sand turned over by the fork. Adding a couple of small blow lug to a black lug bait can be very effective during the winter months.

WHITE RAGWORM

Generally the white ragworm is thought of as the shore match angler's secret bait. They are in fact not easy to dig, need specialist looking after and if you can buy them they are not cheap. So why do the match anglers go to such lengths to get them? The main reason is they will catch fish often when other baits won't; but mainly it's small fish that pleasure anglers aren't bothered about. Small pout are a case in point. Very often they make up the bulk of a competition anglers bag yet if you are fishing for something decent you are trying to avoid these tiny fish. It's the same with small rockling and flounders; they can be caught on white ragworm, but apart from the match angler, who wants them? Large whites, or snakes as they are referred to, are a different proposition. These are only found in a very few places and require a lot of digging to get enough for a fishing session. As they are sometimes more than six inches long they are good for codling, smooth hound and whiting and can be used in the boats as well. A shore angler turning up at a match can hold an advantage if he has a couple of dozen of these beauties in his bait bucket.

SQUID

A box of frozen calamari squid is one of the best standby baits there is. A box can be left in the freezer for several weeks before needed. It's effective on its own and can be used with other baits as a cocktail. All tackle shops keep it in stock although the world stocks have been running low and it is sometimes in short supply. Squid can be used whole for bigger fish such as cod, conger and bull huss. Small strips catch bream, whiting and dogfish, while a combination of squid and worm will catch plaice, gurnard, smooth hound and a host of other species. A cool box should be used to keep your squid in good condition and only take out what you need for the next couple of baits. If they are left out in the sun they soon become ineffective. Don't refreeze squid after a day out fishing, unless it's to be used as groundbait, as it goes pink and catches will suffer as a result.

MACKEREL

Through the summer mackerel becomes the most used bait from the boats. Big shoals move inshore from May onwards and mackerel can be caught on feathers providing ample bait. Mackerel can be used as thin strips for many smaller fish such as bream, gurnard, whiting, pollack and garfish while a large fillet will catch ray, bull huss, dogfish, tope and conger. When cut into flappers, this is when the backbone is cut out leaving the head with the two sides, it catches the larger tope, and big conger. Mackerel is used from the shore in thin strips for garfish in summer and whiting during the colder months. Frozen mackerel will catch dogfish from the beach and it is useful to tip off baits with. From a pier or breakwater, where there's less need to cast, some excellent bass are caught on large mackerel baits, particularly during the autumn.

PEELER CRABS

One of the top baits for certain species is peeler crab. They are not a different species of crab, but a humble shore crab, at that period just before it sheds it shell; so it can grow a little larger each year. Thousands of crabs that are just starting to crack along the edge of the shell are collected each day in estuaries throughout the country with the southwest being the prime spot. Most fish will eat peelers but some are real specialist crab eaters such as smooth hound and bass. These two species like large peeler crab baits but many other fish will feed on small pieces of crab. A peeler crab shell starts to lift as the body inside swells up and this is the best time to use them. The shell is removed along with the feathery lungs, and the crab is cut in half. Two halves can be put on the hook and fixed with a few turns of elastic cotton for the bigger fish while a quarter or half crab will catch flounders, pout, dogfish, bream and all sorts of species. Large smooth hound are caught each year on whole peelers with the shell left on. This tends to keep off the small fish allowing the larger ones to find the bait. Peeler crabs can be kept in the fridge quite successfully for some time as long as they are kept moist. This allows the ones showing signs of peeling to be used first and ensure a stock is always available. A spare fridge in the garage used especially for bait may be a better option to using the wife's indoor fridge. The sight of a crab marching across the bacon or sitting on a pork chop has put many marriages under strain.

HERMIT CRABS

One of the lesser used bait is the hermit crab, mainly because they are not as readily available as peeler crab. They are brilliant bait for smooth hound, and surprisingly are often better after freezing rather than used fresh. Cod are partial to hermit crabs, and other fish like bream will pounce on them. They can only be kept in the fridge for a day or two in aerated water but can be frozen down and stored for some time. The freezing process in fact makes them more attractive to some fish rather than reducing their effectiveness. Push the hook point up through the soft body and out of the underside of the bony body. This holds them firmly in place and presents them in a natural way. If the main claws are large it may be best to break these off to allow the fish to take the crab in one go and make hooking up easier.

PRAWNS

One of the most under-rated baits are prawns and shrimps. They are part of the natural diet of most fish and are readily available in most areas. Prawns can be found in rock pools while shrimps prefer shallow sandy beaches. They can be fished under a float, so they are suspended just off the bottom, for a range of species. Bass have a particular liking to prawns and they patrol round the bottom of stone jetties or the pillars of piers in search of them. Smooth hounds also love a mouthful of prawn and will take them readily when fished on the bottom. Put down a couple of prawns by passing the hook through one of the tail sections from underneath. Prawns will stay on the hook well as long as a gentle cast is made, and the noise they make with their tail will bring smooth hound and bass in from some distance to investigate.

SCALLOP SKIRTS

After a scallop is opened and the tasty centre removed it leaves a tough white muscle all round the shell that is used to open and shut it in the wild. These skirts, as they are referred to, can be removed with a scraping knife and make a good bait for black bream. In the Channel Islands they make big catches of bream on scallop skirts, and because bream are partial to shellfish of any kind they will work in any area bream shoals are found. After removing the skirts from the scallop the resulting bait is a long white strip with some flesh attached. To hook it on push the hook through the tough white muscle then twist it round the hook shank and hook it again. Do this a few times and then with a short length dangling from the bend of the hook lower down. The bites are usually very positive and the fish often hook themselves as the scallop muscle is not easy to pull off the hook.

GARFISH

If you have ever caught a garfish you will have noticed, apart from the way your hands, rod and reel get covered in scales, they give off a pretty strong smell; this makes them a very good bait for an amazing number of species. Firstly, other garfish will take thin strips of it if fished under a float about a metre down; conger eels are another fish that enjoys a garfish chunk. Fillet them off and fish on a long trace while drifting over sand banks and you could catch a turbot, brill and bass. Shore anglers make sure they freeze some down for winter fishing when they become a top bait for whiting. Not only does garfish flesh give off a good scent trail it is a tough flesh that can't be pulled off the hook easily.

LESSER SAND EEL

These are commonly found in shallow inshore water and can be dug with fork or spade at low tide. This small eel-like fish has an extending mouth and only grows to about 20 cm. Can be kept alive in an aerated bucket provided not too many are kept together and are good bait for many fish including bass, pollack, garfish, mackerel and flatfish. As they are available to catch from the shore they are most frequently used in shore fishing. They can be fished under a float from the rocks, piers or marinas for garfish, mackerel and pollack or legered on the bottom for flatfish, dogfish or bass. Take care when baiting them up. A hook through the lower jaw will do fine although some anglers prefer to take the hook through the jaw and nick the hook underneath just behind the vent.

GREATER SAND EEL

Better known as the launce, the greater sand eel can grow to 40 cm and weigh as much as 6 to 8 ounces. They stay buried in the sand during the strongest of the tide run and emerge to form enormous shoals over the sand banks during the slack tide. They can be caught using a set of very small lures, such as Sabikis, with hooks from size 6 down to size 10 or 12. At the end of the lures attach a shiny pirk or Dexter wedge as this seems to attract them to the lures. To keep the launce alive requires a live bait tank with a steady flow of aerated seawater. They are the ultimate bass bait and professional bass anglers go to great lengths to secure enough for a days fishing. The top lip is tougher than the extendable lower lip so this is the best place to hook them. Fish on the drift with the launce on a six to ten foot trace with enough weight to touch bottom. They will also catch turbot and brill fished the same way as above or filleted into long strips and used at anchor. Other fish such as ray, tope, bull huss, pollack, cod and dogfish will find it hard not to be tempted by a tasty sand eel bait.

BLUEYS

Blueys are an imported large, sand eel shaped fish that have been regularly catching fish over the past couple of years. They have an oily flesh with plenty of blood that attracts fish like whiting, dogfish and rays. A good standby bait if other baits like squid or mackerel are scarce.

LIVE BAITS

In the sea everything eats something else, so live baiting is a natural way to catch most fish. Apart from the obvious use of shrimps, prawns, pout, sand eel and mackerel, there are other small fish that can be used effectively. Searching rock pools will produce several small fish that can be used live for bass. Blennies and gobies are a particular favourite of bass, who spend much of their lives hunting for them in gullies and rocky crevices. Scad are another fish that work well as live bait for bass as they are much hardier than mackerel and will stay alive on a hook for a long time. The green shore crab should not be ignored as live bait, as they form much of the diet of smoothhound, bass and cod. Small live mackerel are a top bait for bass when drifted over wrecks or reefs but pout and poor cod work if mackerel are in short supply.

RAZOR FISH

A bait that can make big catches at certain times of the year is the razor fish. They are a long slim shellfish that lives in the sand and can be collected at low tide or after an onshore gale when hundreds can be found washed up on the shore. It's at times like this when they make big catches of flounder and bass. The fish come in to feast on the washed out razors before they can bury themselves back into the sand. Razors can be frozen down very successfully provided they are blanched in boiling water for a few seconds. Frozen razors often catch more fish than fresh ones as they are a little tougher and don't come off when cast out from the shore. There are two ways to catch razor fish. The bigger 'dog' razor can be tempted to the surface by pouring saltwater down its hole in the sand, while the smaller common razor fish can be seen protruding from the sand at low tide, during the night, through the winter months. When low tide occurs in the dark along the south coast, the lights from numerous anglers can be seen zigzagging across the beach as they search for razors.

MUSSEL

Mussels have long been a favourite bait of anglers in the north for cod and coalfish but they are an attractive bait to a wide range of fish. They are easy to obtain as fishmongers always have them on sale or you can collect your own anywhere there is a pier, breakwater or rocks that uncover at low tide. They can be fiddly to open up and get out of their shells and need to be tied onto the hook with some bait elastic but the effort is nearly always worth it. A tasty bunch of mussel will always tempt fish such as bream, codling, whiting, coalfish, wrasse and flatfish. Look out for the larger mussels as they are easier to deal with, having more meat to hook on and plenty of scent to draw the fish in.

HARBOUR RAGWORM

These small ragworm are found in the mud of estuaries or along tidal river banks. They can be dug with a fork but it's a messy business and in all honesty they are of limited use once you've got them. Primarily they are bait for flounders but other species like eel, small bass, mullet and pouting will pick them up. As they are so small they need to be loaded onto a small, fine wire, long shank hook. As many as 10 harbour ragworm slid up the shank of the hook make a decent bait, especially if tipped off with a piece of king ragworm.

COOKED PRAWN

There are several areas of the country where cooked prawn or shrimp will catch fish. The Thames estuary is one place where the flounders have a taste for them. Anglers in the northeast use them for flounders as well but have been adding them to other baits to catch several species including cod, ling and coalfish. Baiting a muppet with a shelled prawn while on the drift has proved another effective way of presenting them.

EEL SEGMENT

Freshwater eel is a very popular bait with tope anglers. A 4 or 5 inch long segment on a 6/0 hook makes a firm and aromatic bait that can be cast uptide easily. The shape of the bait seems to suit the tope and hook ups are very positive with the fish usually hooked in the mouth. Because few other species will take the eel segment it becomes a selective bait for anyone targeting tope.

SWEETCORN

Many fish have become accustomed to sweetcorn and, as they don't seem to fully digest in the body, it finds its way into the sea through the numerous outfall pipes. Dabs have become quite used to a diet of sweetcorn and several pushed onto a size six hook will catch these small flatfish. If not using sweetcorn for bait, slip a yellow bead above a worm bait to represent one, as this will often bring the dabs in to investigate.

MAGGOTS

Although not widely used in sea fishing, maggots have caught plenty of fish in the sea. Mullet can be caught from the shore especially after a gale when seaweed is heaped on the beach and rocks. Any small fish or shellfish caught up in the weed starts rotting and flies lay eggs and maggots start falling in the sea. Mullet will be seen nosing through the weed picking up the maggots. Casting a couple of maggots out near the edge of the weed on a light float rig can produce some good sport. Competition anglers have used them in species hunts to catch small species like blennies, gobies and small wrasse.

BAIT ADDITIVES

There are several bait additives on the market but there is conflicting evidence on whether they are effective or not. Fillets of mackerel dipped in fish oils such as pilchard and sardine before baiting up, will often increase catches of those species that rely heavily on scent like dogfish, bull huss, tope and rays. Specialist additives like Ultrabait have not caught on in a big way but there are a few anglers who have found it has increased their catches. Many anglers have heard of someone spraying WD40 onto their bait before catching some impressive fish and this is not so daft as it sounds. Especially on frozen baits, the WD40 releases some of the enzymes in the flesh increasing the scent trail so there is some credibility to the story. It's still a hard decision whether to spray a perfectly good bait with the stuff hoping it will catch you more fish.

TACKLE

TACKLE

For the beginner, walking into a well-stocked tackle shop can be a very daunting experience as the range on display is vast and appears overwhelming. As long as you know where you want to fish and the likely species you are after the tackle dealer will soon be able to point you in the right direction. To give you a head start we have listed most of the tackle you will come across and give you an idea what it's for. A little knowledge can go a long way and this should give you more confidence to choose the rod, reel and all the rest of the tackle to suit your particular requirements.

SHORE RODS

The first thing a shore rod has to be capable of is casting a weight to the required distance to catch fish. This doesn't always mean a strong rod built for pure distance as there are many areas where a more sensitive rod will be more suitable and produce more fish. Until recently a 12' to 13' rod was ideal for the majority of fishing on open sandy beaches but the latest craze is to go for the continental style of rod that is far longer. You can now purchase rods as long as 5 metres that coupled with a large fixed spool reel can power a weight out big distances with a straight overhead cast. From rocky marks where the requirement is to cast a float rig out a short distance, a 3-metre spinning rod will give good sport. The same sort of rod can be used for casting a small spinner or lure for pollack off the rocks. The longer rods have several advantages though. One is keeping the line above the first line of breakers and preventing the waves pulling it down and breaking the grip of the weight on the sea bed. The longer rod is also more sensitive and bites can be seen more easily.

BOAT RODS

To be a successful boat angler a range of rods will be required to cope with the different styles of fishing and range of species available to catch. In recent years rods have become much more sporting and generally longer to meet the needs of the match angler and particularly the arrival of braid. Braid doesn't stretch so the rods need to be more flexible to counter this, as a fast moving fish will rip the hook straight out if there is no give in either rod or line. For bigger fish such as conger, large cod and blonde ray, a more powerful 30lb class rod measuring around seven feet in length is heavy enough. For most general fishing a 12lb to 20lb class rod around eight feet in length will cope with fish such as tope, smooth hound, the smaller rays and cod. For anything smaller use an even lighter rod such as one of the many 10' multi-tip rods that make fishing for bream, pollack and wrasse such a pleasure. In shallow areas with strong tides a 10 feet long uptide rod will be needed. This is long enough to make smooth casts uptide and be powerful enough to play the fish in.

DOWNTIDE RODS

For the bigger species such as congers, tope and

ray, a rod of about 7 to 8 feet is ideal and should be in the 20lb to 30lb class. The exception to this is tackling the large common skate when a 50lb class rod would be needed. For the rest of the species caught down tide longer rods are now the modern trend, with multi-tip rods a popular choice. These give the option of having one rod with but with three different weight tips that can cope with very light weights up to a pound of lead in the stronger tides. These multi-tip rods have generally been around three metres in length giving great sport with fish like black bream. On the international scene this has been taken a step further with rods as long as five metres being regularly used in major competitions. Although unwieldy in a boat, with several other anglers on board, they show up the smallest of bites and many fish have hooked themselves before they know it. These long rods are usually combined with a large fixed spool reel rather than the multiplier, and have proved very successful.

UPTIDE RODS

The modern uptide rod needs to be powerful enough to cast an 8oz lead but still maintain sensitivity in the tip to show every bite. The majority of uptide rods on the market are around 10' in length and some have an integral butt, originally designed by Michael McManus of Conoflex. This allows the butt to be extended for casting and with a twist and push, shortened when winding in a fish. This works well where thornback ray are caught as the long butt of the normal uptide rod needs to be held under the armpit, making leverage on a heavy thornback difficult. With the integral butt type of rod, by giving a quick twist, about a foot of rod will push into the butt making it shorter, the rod can then be placed in a butt pad giving maximum leverage.

MULTIPLIER REELS

The multiplier reel is widely used in boat fishing as it copes with heavy loads and has a reliable drag system. They are well engineered, smooth running and are used for both down tide and uptide fishing. Some multipliers have a lever drag that can be pushed forwards to increase the pressure on the fish while most other reels rely on a star drag system on the side of the reel. Again this can be turned to increase the pressure making it harder for the fish to strip off line. In strong tides and fast flowing water a large multiplier is the only reel to get the weight back without too much of a struggle especially when a big fish is on the end. Small multipliers are the choice of many boat anglers for bream fishing. The same reels are used for long distance casting and most general fishing from the shore. They need to be filled up with 300 yards of 15lb mono and have a 20' leader of 30lb to 50lb breaking strain.

FIXED SPOOL REELS

A decade ago fixed spool reels on boats were very much in the minority and joked at as being an 'egg whisk'. Since the Italians have won the CIPES World

Boat Championships several times using fixed spool reels at venues where they were not expected to work there has been a big change of heart. Nowadays all the top anglers will be using fixed spool reels for uptide fishing and light down tiding. The one area where they don't cope so well is fishing for the larger species such as ray and conger. The fixed spool reel is much easier to cast very small weights if trying to find pollack and garfish from a boat. On the beach many beginners choose a fixed spool to start with as the likelihood of an over run or birdsnest is minimal. Care must be taken to see that the bale arm stays over as it can cause a snap off if it flicks back on its own during the cast.

TACKLE BOXES

As there is such a lot of equipment a boat angler may be called upon to use during a day out a good tackle box is important. It should have a tray inside so that all the bits and pieces like spare line, rig wallets, knives, swivels and hooks can be found quickly while the bottom of the box should have room for waterproofs, lunch, flask and some reserve equipment like pirks, shads and booms. A sturdy strap with some sort of cushioning saves the shoulders if there's a long walk to the boat. The shore angler has different needs and many boxes incorporate small trays for bait and others have a seat with a back rest built in. There are a few tackle boxes that have wheels for easy pulling along promenades and piers. Being waterproof is a main requirement and it's easier to carry a box with the strap coming out at the middle of each side rather than at the back of the box. Pick up a tackle box that has the straps coming out at the back and the whole thing tips forward and spills everything inside.

RIG WALLETS

Keeping lots of ready-made rigs ready to use and easy to find prompted sea anglers to put various things to use like a photo album until a purpose made rig wallet came on the scene. These canvas or plastic holders with up to 20 clear envelopes inside proved ideal to keep all manner of rigs in, including three-boom paternoster in the larger envelopes. It didn't completely eradicate tangles as the rigs were taken out for use but this is how anglers have kept their rigs for the past decade or so but now there is a new idea that has caught on in a big way. Rig wallets are still popular for certain bits of tackle but for storing rigs the rig spool has taken over in a big way.

RIG SPOOLS

A rig spool is a firm plastic or foam spool that the rig can be wound round. The hooks can be pressed into the spool as they are wound on then the loop at the end held in place with a pin. To get the rig off without tangles just take out the pin and unwind it releasing each hook as you come to it. Clip a weight on the bottom swivel and you are ready to go. To store these spools the local do-it-yourself provided the answer with the clear plastic tool box made into small compartments for screws, nails, nuts and bolts. You can find one to fit the spools and then it's a matter of labelling each one so it can be found easily. Some spools can be written on while other people may mark the lid of the tool box.

RUNNING BOOMS

Running booms are widely used in boat fishing when fishing for species that take the bait then move off quickly such as bass, tope or rays or back off like conger eels. They are made of plastic tubing with a weight holder on them. The main line runs through the tube with a bead slipped on the line and sturdy swivel or swivel link on the end that the trace is attached to. The idea is that the weight stays where it is and the fish can move off with the bait feeling little resistance.

FIXED BOOMS

The fixed boom is used for smaller species that don't run off with the bait and will often hook themselves as they pull against the fixed line. The boom can be fished anywhere from the bottom to several feet up the line. It serves to prevent tangles as the bait is lowered down. Up to three fixed booms can be fitted above the weight when fishing for smaller species and this is referred to as a paternoster rig. If the trace to the hook is kept shorter than the boom it will prevent any chance of tangles.

FLYING COLLAR

The flying collar is the name given to the fixed boom used when fishing for pollack over the deepwater wrecks. Traces as long as 4 metres are used for this type of fishing with an artificial eel or a live sand eel. The flying collar keeps the trace away from the main line as it's dropped down keeping tangles to a minimum.

BREAKAWAY LEADS

One of the best inventions ever for the shore angler was the breakaway lead. They are a weight with wires that can be pushed into place creating a grapnel that keeps the tackle in place in the tide. Then when it's time to be pulled in the wires unclip to allow the weight to be pulled in easily.

GRAPNEL LEADS

Before the arrival of breakaway leads the grapnel kept the weight anchored well but were difficult to recover. The grapnel has wires that are fixed in place as the lead is poured into a weight mould. The wires are then bent into shape and sometimes it is hard to retrieve them. They are still used in rough weather or in strong tides and boat anglers prefer them for uptiding.

WATCH LEADS

The old fashioned watch shaped weight are made for drift fishing from the boats when flatfish are the target. The bumps on the weight kick up puffs of sand as they are pulled along the bottom. This attracts plaice, brill and turbot to investigate, bringing them close to the bait, which they will grab at as it goes by.

SWIM FEEDER LEADS

It's now possible to purchase a lead weight with a small swim feeder cage on. These can be filled with groundbait of some sort and cast out easily. The idea is to attract the fish to the hook bait nearby. Mashed mackerel or old worms pushed into the plastic swim feeder will send off a good scent trail bringing fish in from some distance.

MONO

The most universal fishing line over the past 30 years has been nylon or monofilament. Mostly mass-produced in USA and Germany it has been the standard line for just about every type of fishing. The main reason for its popularity is economy, reliability and its abrasive resistance. The consistency of manufacture for lines that can be purchased in just 2lb breaking strain and in spools of up to a mile long defies belief. Economy spools tend to be stronger than the stated breaking strain on the packet so if the line is for breaking records it must have the tag IGFA rated. This is a sign that the line has been thoroughly tested and will break within the stated breaking strain and not above it. For example if a claim is put in for a fish for the 20lb line class record, an economy 20lb line may test out at 25lb breaking strain while the 20lb IGFA rated line will probably break at 18lb to 19lb breaking strain.

BRAID

Since the introduction of braided line it has

transformed the world of sea fishing. The non-stretch property, the incredible bite detection and the low diameter compared to similar breaking strength mono has seen a fantastic increase in sales. Because of the low diameter, less weight is needed to hold bottom in a tide run and even in deep water a small bite can be felt clearly, while it may well have been missed on mono line. There are some reservations over braid, and one is the price. It certainly isn't cheap, and it's not so abrasive-resistant as mono, so over rough ground a mono leader should be used to take the hard knocks. With fast fighting fish the lack of stretch in the line can mean the hook hold breaking free, especially if the rod doesn't have a really soft tip. If the braid gets tangled with another angler line using mono it can be difficult to separate. Generally, though, braid has taken over as the first choice for main line.

FLUOROCARBON

Another recent addition to the sea angler's tackle is the arrival of fluorocarbon line for traces. This line is designed not to reflect light, and this means it's virtually invisible in water giving anglers more chance of fooling the fish to take a bait. Fluorocarbon line is a bit stiffer than ordinary mono but this can be an advantage when making rigs as it's less likely to tangle.

HOOKS

There is an incredible range of hooks for sea fishing ranging from tiny fine wire hooks to meaty 14/0's for large shark and skate. The choice from this vast range can soon be whittled down to which bait is being used and which species are being targeted. This mention of target fish is relevant as it nearly always pays to have in mind what the likely fish will be caught. We can't always be sure of what will be hooked as that's one of the great thrills of sea fishing, but it is best to start with something in mind. There are long shank hooks, short shank hooks, bait holders, barbless, thin wire and extra strong. Then there are the shapes of hooks such as offset, circle and semi-circle to confuse the beginner even more. The way to choose is to go for a sharp hook such as a chemically sharpened one and start smaller rather than larger. The old adage that a small hook will catch a large fish but a large hook won't catch a small one is correct. This means using a large hook will cut your chances of landing anything other than a large fish. This is fine if you are after one large fish but most anglers want to catch several fish. For beginners to boat fishing an ideal hook would be a size 1 or 1/0 long shank hook. This will catch just about everything. For a pier or shore angler a size 2 or 4 would probably give the most sport.

HOOK PARTS

You wouldn't think a hook has seven defining parts, but it does. These consist of the eye, shank, throat, gape, barb and the point. The seventh is more abstract as it's the distance between the point and the bend and called the throat. All of these seven items can be different on each range of hooks.

The Point

The point can be a knife-edge, which is found in more expensive hooks used for bigger species, where the mouths are tougher and the cutting knife-edge is needed help to penetrate the bony area. The regular hook most manufacturers produce is the spear point that is rounded on the inside and flat on the outside. The match angler's favourite hook is the needle point. These are made from finer wire and are usually sold as chemically sharpened. The ultra-sharp point will penetrate into anything, especially good for hooking small, shy biting species.

The Eye

The most common hook eye is the ringed eye that is made by turning the end of the shank over and forming a circle. These are usually on the cheaper hooks and care must be taken to see that the end closes up otherwise the line can slip out and it can catch on other lines when fishing in close quarters like on a charter boat. When this join is fused together to eliminate this possible gap it is called a brazed eye.

Then there is a needle eye that is created by removing an oval hole in the top of the shank with no join at all. This ensures there are no weak spots and nowhere to catch on anything. If you prefer to whip your own hooks, the spade end hooks are the ones to choose. Many ready-made bait catching rigs use this method to fix the lures on with.

The Shank

All hooks are made in different lengths and the shank determines the length. Why are hooks made in different lengths? Because some fish have very sharp teeth and a long shaft will cut down the chances of them biting through the hook snood. Some baits need to be slid up the shank to be presented properly so again a long shank would be best. Short shank hooks can be used where baits aren't threaded up the line but just hooked once to wave enticingly in the tide.

The Throat

The throat of the hook is the depth of hook from the tip of the point to the bend in the hook. It's not something many anglers are aware of and probably will never give another thought to.

The Gape

The gape refers to the width of the hook from the point to the shank. In some big boat competitions, for example in Norway, there are restrictions on the width of the gape. This came about because anglers using a treble hook on a pirk found they could foul hook fish by using a wide gape treble and it was deemed as unsporting.

The Bend

Surprisingly, most hooks have different shaped bends. Generally they conform to a set pattern as any extreme can weaken the holding power of the hook. Apart from the regular shaped bends there are wide gape hooks used by many shore anglers and of course semi-circle and circle hooks have a much-changed shape to them.

The Barb

To stop the hook falling out of the mouth of the fish a barb is cut into the shank that acts like a non-return valve. This is very effective for catching fish but in the modern conservational sense they can harm some fish. This is a result of the difficulty the angler has to remove the barbed hook. More and more clubs and organisations are trying barbless hooks to see if the survival rate is improved. Conger eels and dogfish are two species that are released at the side of the boat. Provided the line is kept tight during the playing of the fish it won't come off a barbless hook, but it makes it so much easier to flick the hook out when it comes to the surface using a T-bar.

Offset hooks

The regular hooks above can be straight or bent. This doesn't in this case refer to their sexuality. A straight hook is just that: a hook with a straight shank. The bent one is referred to as offset. This is when the point and barb are bent away from the shank at a slight angle to make the hooking of the fish more reliable. Some anglers swear by them and will go to the lengths of bending perfectly good straight hooks, while others are convinced the straight hook will penetrate more powerfully.

Circle hooks

Longliners have used circle hooks for many years and it's easy to see why. If a fish takes the bait and runs off with it the circle hook pulls out of the gullet and lodges in the side of the mouth. This means it's an easy job to remove the hooks. If an angler wants to use circle hooks they work best for the fish that pick up a bait and runs with it such as bass, tope and smooth hound. A strike is not necessary when using a circle hook as it pulls into the side of the mouth as the fish moves off. The one difficulty is baiting the hook as it's not quite so easy as it is with a normal shaped hook.

SWIVEL LINKS

At the end of the main line it requires a link that can be clipped to whatever trace or rig is being used and the most widely used is the swivel link. It's a combination of a swivel that allows the trace to twist round without breaking and an easy to open link to use as a connector. Again, the angler has a good choice and it comes down to personal preference. The American swivel link is popular for boat anglers as it has no bits sticking out to catch other lines, but shore anglers need a much stronger one as they are always concerned about snap offs and the danger from flying leads if one comes off.

ROD RESTS

Shore anglers need somewhere to put their rod while waiting for a bite, and the most efficient rod rest is a tripod. They are now made with extra clips and hooks for hanging spare traces and maybe a bucket on. The monopod is used to a lesser extent as it needs to be pushed well into the sand or shingle to hold the rod upright in any sort of a wind. Boat anglers sometimes need a rod rest or holder where the boat has a chrome railing all round. If not the rod is forever sliding along into the next angler's rod. A clever and light weight holder is a Velcro one that wraps round the railing, and another is a shaped rounded plastic that grips the rail and has a groove in to take the rod.

RIG WALLETS

One of the most useful items for sea anglers is a rig wallet. They have a canvas or plastic cover with up to 20 clear plastic envelopes in that can each hold a different rig. It's so easy to flick through the wallet to find the particular one required as conditions or requirements change during the day. By having several wallets they can be used for example with three hook traces in one, two hook traces in another. A wallet can be kept with traces for certain fish such as heavy traces for conger or sets of feathers for mackerel. Use one of the smaller hook wallets to keep the hooks handy and visible rather than in several plastic containers. The more organised you are the easier the fishing becomes.

BEADS

There are all sorts of uses for a packet of multi-coloured beads. Slip one on your line before tying on a swivel link will stop the top eye being damaged or the swivel jamming in it. When using a running boom put one between the boom and the end swivel; this stops the swivel damaging the end of the boom. A trace with several coloured beads will attract plaice, and a wrasse rig with yellow, orange or red beads catches more fish.

Mini beads

Mini or micro beads are used in trace making for both shore and boat rigs. Boat anglers employ them when using two-way beads to make a paternoster rig. On the main trace line they can be used either side of the bead before a crimp is used to hold the bead in place. Alternatively, if a knot is used instead of a crimp, a micro bead will prevent the knot slipping through the hole in the bead. When the hook snood is pushed through the bead the other way a micro bead can be slipped on the line and a knot tied to hold it in place. Again the micro bead prevents the knot getting pulled through the bead. Shore anglers use them on many rigs usually in conjunction with crimps holding swivels in place. The beads allow the swivel to revolve on the trace line efficiently.

Floating beads

The use of floating beads is not widespread but there are certain circumstances where they can help: keeping the bait out the way of crabs in estuaries for example. They can give a bit of movement to a large bait by making it a bit buoyant and allowing it to wave about in the tide when down tiding for cod. Fishing for garfish is another occasion where a floating bead can be used to keep the bait near the surface. Generally it's down to the individual anglers own ingenuity to make the most of things like floating beads and try a few experiments with them.

Fluoro beads

Many anglers use green fluorescent beads on their

rigs believing it will send out some sort of light when on the bottom – definitely worth using in the evening starting at dusk, but they seem to work the rest of the day as well. Dogfish and bull huss seem drawn to them so it's worth adding one to a bottom rig as it can't do much harm.

SEQUINS

Shore anglers use sequins on many of their traces – particularly when fishing for flatfish. The shiny holographic disc is so light it doesn't affect casting but seems to attract inquisitive fish like flounders and plaice. It's possible they may be more effective in shallow or clear water but there's no harm in trying them in other conditions as they don't compromise the action of the trace or put the fish off.

SPOONS AND FLASHERS

The original flounder spoon was just that. The handle was cut off a desert spoon and a hole drilled each end of the spoon part. They were then attached just above the hook and worked in the tide to catch flounders in estuaries. The same rig proved to catch fish from boats where the tide could work the spoon making it lift and turn. Modern spoons are a little more refined and smaller flashers made of shiny plastic can be purchased that can be used on all sorts of rigs. Cod are another species that are drawn to the sight and movement of some sort of spoon or flasher while it makes no difference to some species.

DROP NET

Pier fishermen have the problem of getting a fish up onto the pier after they have hooked and played it. Lifting any fish weighing over a couple of pounds will either break the line or pull the hook free. The answer is to use a drop net. This is a round net about the size of a bicycle wheel with a thin but strong rope attached at three points of the rim. The net is lowered into the water until it is about 6 inches below the surface so the fish can be manoeuvred over it. The net is then lifted steadily and the fish drops into the net for safe recovery.

LANDING NET

As many anglers like to return any unwanted fish to the sea the use of gaffs has virtually died out. A landing net can be used for all fish including the larger species like ray, smooth hound and bull huss. Many charter skippers have had extra large landing nets made so they can lift out a conger, weigh the fish and then return it unhurt to the sea.

T BAR

Fish like conger, tope and dogfish that are to be returned are often not brought on-board but are T-barred at the side of the boat. This involves holding the line tight with the left hand while the bend on the T-bar is slid down to the hook with the right hand. Then the line is pulled down by the left hand as the T-bar pulls upwards on the hook that comes free allowing the fish to drop back into the water.

This saves handling the fish and means they can't injure themselves by thrashing about in the boat.

GLOVES

Charter skippers and boat owners should always have a pair of gloves handy in case a line gets stuck on the bottom. Modern braids are so strong and thin that they can cause a serious cut if pulled with bare hands. With a stout pair of gloves the line can be wound round a couple of turns and broken free. Gloves are also useful when retrieving the anchor rope, especially in the colder months.

KNIVES

Apart from the obvious need for knives to cut up the bait, and maybe filleting fish at the end of the day, many small boat owners keep one in a holder close to the back of the boat. This is in case of an emergency like getting a rope round the propeller. If you need to search round for a knife it could be too late to prevent a problem becoming a disaster.

CRIMPS

A crimp is a thin metal tube that can be slid into the line and pinched with pliers or a crimping tool to hold beads or swivels in place. They are also used on heavy traces such as those needed for conger fishing to hold the hooks and swivels on without using knots. Thick line like the 150lb mono used for conger traces is very difficult to knot and the crimps make a much neater job.

BAIT NEEDLES

If you have difficulty getting fine baits like white ragworm, blow lug and small ragworm on to the hook you should be try a bait needle. Push the point of the needle through the head of the worm and thread it up the needle. Repeat the process until you have several worms threaded on; now put the point of the hook into the other end of the needle that is hollowed out to take the point; now keeping the line to the hook tight, hold it in one hand against the end of the needle and with the other hand push the worms up and round onto the hook and up the shank. Sounds fiddly but in practice it is a fast way to get good bait presentation. Between casts you can get several needles baited ready for the next time you pull in.

BAIT DROPPER

Even fishing from a boat it often pays to put some groundbait down although it would be wrong to put it down in the full run of tide. Several methods have been devised to get the groundbait to the bottom such as a plastic bag with a weight tied inside. As it hits the bottom the line pulls the weight up and turns the bag inside out letting the groundbait out. A more efficient way is to use a purpose made metal bait dropper such as The Edge. This has a large lead on the bottom that pushes the dropper open as it hits the bottom. After using this equipment, gutted fish are often found to contain the cut up material put down as groundbait, proving it works.

RIG GLUE

Braided line is very slippery and badly tied knots can pull out. It pays to put a blob of glue such as super glue or rig glue on any knots just to give that added security. Leader knots between braid and mono, especially for shore fishing, benefit from using a bit of glue if only from the safety point of view.

FISH

Here are a few tips on the baits and the methods of targeting the most popular fish caught round our coastline.

BASS

The most sort after fish for sea anglers in the UK is the hard fighting and impressive looking bass. They can be caught from shore, pier and boat, on a wide range of baits and lures, using several different angling methods. Pier anglers can catch them on float-fished prawns or live small fish such as pout and poor cod. A mackerel head fished close to a breakwater or the piles of the pier will catch some very large bass in late summer and early autumn. Shore anglers catch bass in the surf with lugworm, shellfish or crab baits, the best time just after a storm. From rocky coastlines bass will be foraging for crabs, prawns and small fish like blennies and rockling. Any of these can be used as bait but use a rotten bottom of some sort as you need to fish in the gullies between the rocks. Casting lures from beach, rocks and pier will catch bass, especially when they are chasing white bait or mackerel close inshore. Boat anglers are fortunate to be able to catch bass in several different ways: live mackerel, sand eel, pout, scad or pout drifted over wrecks or reefs will catch bass of all sizes; if no live bait is available an imitation sand eel or shad can often catch just as many in tide races and over reefs. Bass will happily take mackerel strip, squid or lugworm fished on the bottom and shoals of school bass competing with each other for food will fall to a set of hokkai lures.

Slow growing

The drawback with bass is they are a very slow growing species and a double figure fish will be as much as 15 years old. This means they are very susceptible to over-fishing as it takes a long time to build the stocks back up. The other problem is the minimum landing size (MLS) for commercial catches is set too low. At 36cm a bass is not mature enough to breed so they never have a chance to reproduce themselves. If a slight increase in the MSL to 40cm was made (still only a fish of around one and a half pounds) it would make a big difference, while a move to 45cm would ensure they had spawned at least once and there would be more bass for the commercial fishery and recreational anglers.

COD

The second favourite fish for anglers are cod, as they grow to be quite big and are delicious when caught and cooked fresh. Although cod have always been considered a winter fish from the shore, there are still plenty to be caught throughout the year from the boats. For shore anglers a decent codling represents probably the biggest fish they are ever likely to land. They will feed on lugworm, squid and shellfish and during darkness in the winter months will come inshore to within casting range. Best bait is three or four lugworm tipped off with a thin strip of squid and cast as far as possible.

Boat anglers will catch on the same bait while fishing the inshore marks in autumn and winter while for the very big cod the bait should be stepped up to two or three whole squid. In summer boat anglers have more options as they can catch cod over the wrecks on a variety of lures including jelly worms, shad, redgills, feathers and leadheads. Many cod are caught uptiding as this method ensures the bait is fixed to the bottom so the cod can follow the scent trail. A good bunch of black lug or yellow tails will catch plenty of cod from the fast running and shallow estuaries such as the Thames, the Mersey and the Bristol Channel.

FLATFISH

There are several main species of flatfish the UK sea angler will come across, with the plaice, dab, sole, flounder, turbot and brill the most likely. They are all bottom feeders and tackle required to catch them reflects this. While it would be unusual to catch turbot and brill from the shore all the rest of the flatfish family can be caught from the shore and pier. Flatfish are renowned for their delicious flavour and are all sort after food for the kitchen.

DABS

The smallest of the flatfish is the dab, but it is a fun fish to catch on light tackle and will take a range of baits. Found over sand and gravel, they feed on worms, shrimp, shellfish and will chase sprats through the winter months. They move inshore in vast numbers late in the year and can be caught from the shore through until the spring. Tackle up with size six hooks baited with frozen lugworm as these have proved to be the best bait for dabs.

FLOUNDER

Flounders are in peak condition during autumn and winter as they move offshore to spawn early in the New Year. Any estuary or harbour holds flounders and they mainly feed on ragworm and crab. Where there are crabs about waiting to steal the bait use a big bunch of ragworm or even half a peeler crab. In some areas a bunch harbour ragworm is the best bait and a flounder spoon can increase catches.

PLAICE
Plaice move inshore during the spring when they will be rather thin after spawning. They build up their condition through the year so the best plaice are taken later in the year. They will feed in daytime on lugworm, ragworm and sand eel. Tip off worm baits with a long strip of squid as this acts as an attractor.

SOLE
Small hooks baited with tiny pieces of ragworm or lugworm will catch sole if fished from dusk through to darkness, the best time being late summer into autumn. Sole are a surprisingly strong fish and will bend their tail up as they are being retrieved making them difficult to land.

TURBOT AND BRILL
Turbot and brill are not widely available even to the boat angler but certain areas over sand banks where there are shoals of sand eels will be the most likely spots to pick one up. Drifting the banks with a long strip of mackerel or launce on 4/0 hook and a six-foot long trace should bring success but patience is required. If a bite is felt, give the fish several yards of line before lifting into it.

POLLACK
Boat anglers have the best chance of catching big pollack but shore anglers will catch some lively specimens from piers and rocky marks. The most

popular way to catch pollack from a boat is using the long trace and a flying collar, baited with a live sand eel, ragworm, strip of mackerel or a jelly worm. The flying collar is a fixed boom that helps keep the long trace from tangling on the way to the bottom. Once on the bottom the rig is then wound up steadily to about 35 turns up as the boat drifts over the wreck. The pollack follow the bait and will grab it and dive back to the wreck giving some heart stopping moments as the line peels off the reel. Shore anglers can catch pollack by spinning a small lure over rocks or weed beds or float fishing a live sand eel, ragworm or mackerel strip over the same area.

WRASSE

Another species that can be caught from shore, pier and boat is the colourful ballan wrasse. They are mostly caught on ragworm in heavily weeded rocky areas and are very territorial. From piers and rocks a simple paternoster or a float-fished ragworm will catch wrasse, but the larger specimens will be hard to get out from their rocky lairs. Very often a big ballan wrasse will come out, grab the bait and dive back into the safety of the rocks, resulting in a snap off. Limpets, mussels and any other shellfish will catch wrasse, although some of these baits are rather soft and may need fixing on with elastic cotton. Peeler crabs are another good bait for wrasse with small pieces proving very effective for the smaller species and a large whole one ideal if looking for a specimen ballan wrasse. Small whole shore crabs will also pick out the bigger specimens. In the boats wrasse will be found on most reefs with the ballan wrasse more likely on the inshore marks.

SMALL WRASSE

Cuckoo wrasse are often caught further out than the larger ballans and will take a strip of mackerel as well as the ragworm. The male and female cuckoo are quite different in appearance; the female is orange with three dark blotches at the base of the dorsal fin near the tail; the male is resplendent with a bright blue head and back and yellow on the sides and underneath. Another member of the wrasse family that may be encountered fishing from the shore or dinghies close to shore is the corkwing, which has a dark curved blotch behind the eye and a black spot at the base of its tail; there are blue and orange lines running from the mouth towards the eye. The rock cook is only tiny and has a dark band on its tail and has blue along the dorsal fin. The goldsinny is another wrasse that only grows to about 6 inches; it is pale orange when caught with a black spot on the top of the tail and another at the front of the dorsal fin. Even more unusual are the baillons wrasse but they can be identified by the single black spot in the middle of the dorsal fin and the orange fins. The body is quite mottled when first caught with a dark blotch on the base of the tail. If targeting these small fish in match conditions reduce the size of hooks to as small as a size 10 and bait with tiny pieces of ragworm. Another tip for wrasse fishing is to keep the traces very short and have one of the baits very close to the lead. Catches can be improved by using a weight painted yellow or red.

BLACK BREAM

One of the most exciting sea fish to catch is the black bream. Although there are very few places where they can be caught from the shore, the pier is probably the most likely place to pick up a decent one. Squid is their number one bait with mackerel strip, worm and crab also catching plenty of fish. On light tackle the bream will give a sharp bite and put up a good fight as it darts about very quickly. In the boats the small bream can strip off baits set for other fish while the big bream will sometimes take large baits set for ray, huss or congers. Bream will feed off the bottom so a paternoster can be effective and dropping down ground bait will keep a shoal feeding near the boat. When fishing from a boat, set the hooks with one 0.30m off the bottom, the next one at around 0.60m and put one a lot higher, at as much as 1.50m. Bream will rise well up in the water, particularly at slack tide, and this higher hook will indicate if they are feeding well up. To get the best out of black bream use a long soft rod and enjoy the sport they give.

OTHER BREAM

As the seawater has warmed up in recent years other bream have begun to show up in ever increasing numbers. One in particular is the gilthead bream that seems to favour estuaries where it will feed on shrimps, prawns, mussels and crabs. They are a powerful fish, grow bigger than the black bream and give the angler some exciting sport when hooked. They are found in most west-country rivers in late summer and also anywhere mussels are commercially farmed. Tackle should be a spinning rod with a fixed spool and best bait is a prawn fished on a simple running leger through a ball lead. The couches bream, red bream and Pandora are much less widespread but likely to be encountered while fishing for black bream.

GREY MULLET

One of the most frustrating and difficult fish to catch from the shore are grey mullet. They frequent harbours and estuaries all round our coastline and require a certain guile to tempt them to take a bait. There are in fact three species of mullet: the thick lipped, thin lipped and the golden grey. The main target for anglers are the thick lipped that can be seen in large shoals cruising round boats, piles and sea walls. They can be caught on bread but need to be brought on the feed by ground baiting. This can be just a matter of regular feeding with crusts or a bit more specialised by mixing bread and fish oil that can be spooned in at intervals to keep the fish in the area. Once the mullet start to feed, a free lined floating crust or a piece of dough squeezed gently on to a small hook, with enough split shot to take the bait slowly down through the water, will both reap rewards. As mullet are very nervous feeders, a Fluorocarbon line of around 6lb breaking strain and a size 6 hook are all that's required, matched to a 10 ft or 12 ft carp rod and a small fixed spool reel. Even after a mullet is hooked the odds of landing a fish in excess of 5lbs are not good as they will dive for any obstructions and smash the line.

OTHER MULLET

The thin-lipped mullet will take a moving bait and the most successful way of catching one is to remove the treble hook off a small Mepps spinner and replace with a single hook. This should be baited with a small piece of ragworm and cast ahead of any fish and gently wound back so they will see the flash of the spoon and come to investigate. Golden grey mullet are not so widely distributed and again need a different approach. They are found during the summer on sandy beaches where they will move in with the tide across the warm sand. Use a bunch of harbour ragworm or maddies on a small hook and cast them a short distance into the incoming tide to find the fish.

RED MULLET

The red mullet is not included in the mullet section because it isn't strictly a mullet — it's a goat fish. The striped red mullet is the one found in increasing numbers along the south coast taking baits put down for bream, gurnard and other small fish. It has three yellow stripes along its sides; the plain red mullet is generally found in much deeper water. They both have extended barbels that are used to locate small fish and shellfish in the sand.

SHARK

There are sharks round our coast but they are mainly well out to sea giving little access to shore anglers. Boat anglers need to be well organised to take on shark and it's probably best to book a specialist charter boat for those wanting to have the chance to battle with one. Blue, porbeagle, thresher and mako sharks are all regular visitors, with blue shark the one most often caught by anglers.

SMOOTH HOUND

One of the most exciting and sporting fish from UK waters are the common and starry smooth hound. Both are caught in similar ways and can be targeted as one species. They arrive in early spring to feed up on peeler and hermit crabs; these are the two top baits to catch them on although later in the summer they also take a cocktail of squid and ragworm. Smooth hound like a good tide run and in areas like the Thames estuary and the Bristol channel an efficient way to catch them is to cast uptide with a grapnel lead. Shore anglers can enjoy some brilliant sport with fish to double figures from certain areas such as Selsey Bill, Sussex, where big catches are made each year.

SPURDOG

Every spring large shoals of spurdog used to invade the south coast and it was difficult to avoid them. In recent years the shoals have been decimated by over fishing and catches have declined to the extent a good spurdog is news. The spurdog, as the name suggests has two very sharp spurs on its back just ahead of the dorsal fins. If the fish is to be retained these spurs should be removed. They grow to 20 lbs and put up a spirited fight when hooked. As they are a deepwater fish the most efficient rig is a paternoster with short hook snoods that won't tangle on the drop. Inshore in the spring they can be caught on a short flowing trace with a 3/0 hook baited with mackerel or squid.

BULL HUSS

Another species of the dogfish family that are regularly caught around our coastline are bull huss. They are a beige coloured fish shaped like a blunt nosed shark with numerous black spots over the whole body; they can grow into double figures and will feed on fish baits, crabs and worms. Their skin is very abrasive so a strong trace is needed with a 2/0 or 3/0 hook baited with mackerel or squid.

DOGFISH

One of the most prolific fish around our coasts is the humble dogfish. Although similar in shape to the bull huss they are much smaller — rarely growing to more than 3lbs. Baits can be any fish bait, worms or peeler crab, and hooks no bigger than a 1/0 are needed. The spots on the dogfish are much smaller than the bull huss and the nasal flap is one piece while the bull huss has two quite separate flaps.

MACKEREL

For most anglers the mackerel is a bait fish but for pier anglers they can be a lot of fun to catch. A set of feathers or small lures will catch them as the shoals move inshore. Mackerel arrive in early summer and leave in late autumn depending on the water temperature. One of the most enjoyable ways to catch them is to use a light spinning rod and bait a thin strip of fish bait on a size six hook suspended about six feet under a float.

GARFISH

During the summer and autumn it's great fun fishing for garfish on light tackle. These sporting little fish are the nearest we have to a game fish and will leap clear of the water and fight all the way in. A garfish looks like an eel with a long beak. It is green on the back and silver underneath and when cooked its bones go green but the flesh is very tasty and safe to eat.

Pier rig

Best method to catch them from a pier is to fish a strip of mackerel under a float. One of the most successful rigs is made up like this: tie a stop knot about three feet up the main line; then slide on a fairly large float followed by a small ball weight, a bead and a swivel. A trace of between three and five feet with a size six hook on is then fixed to the swivel and baited with a thin strip of mackerel. When casting the float will sit on the ball lead but will slide up to the stop knot as it lands in the water.

Shore rig

The pier rig can be used off the shore but can tangle if long casts are attempted. There are two other methods to try for garfish from the shore. The first is when using a normal two-hook bottom rig with breakaway lead. The rig is cast out and the line tightened up before another short trace and hook is clipped to the line. Lift the rod up high and the trace will slide down to the water where it will catch fish near the surface. A swan shot should be used to keep the bait a few feet down, as seagulls will soon be after the bait if it's too near the surface. Another rig that makes casting easy and stops tangles is to use a bubble float half filled with water. The float is fixed at the end of the trace and the water gives enough weight to make casting effortless. Two hooks can be fixed above the float on traces far enough apart that they don't tangle. A swan shot on each will ensure they hang below the surface. At the top of the trace a couple of floating beads should be attached so the rig doesn't sink. The whole rig from bubble float to floating beads should be no more than 6 feet in length so it can be cast easily. When cast the bubble float goes first and then acts similar to a long line when in the water. Giving the rig a short tug now and again can attract attention from the gars.

Boat rig

From the boat, the pier rig is the best option as it

can be floated away from the boat on the tide or flicked away far enough to clear the boat. If the tide is running strongly then a free line bait is preferred to using the float. The bait can be fed out in the tide and bites can be felt as the bait drifts down tide. A small ball lead or something similar can be added if the bait is not sinking far enough. Generally garfish feed from 3 to 6 feet below the surface but will take bait off the surface provided a seagull hasn't got it first. This is why it's best to keep the bait a few feet down.

WHITING
Though autumn and winter the most prolific species caught in the UK is the whiting. They can be a real pest sometimes when they are stripping large baits set for cod, but in reality more whiting will be caught than anything else through the cod season. One way to target them is to use baited hokkai or silver shrimp lures especially if they have some red on them. Bait can be mackerel, squid or worm and over the slack tide can feed voraciously. Most areas where there are large whiting shoals the fish will be no more than a couple of pounds but a few places have some quality fish of up to four pounds. Here a Wessex type rig with one hook on the bottom and one up the line with 1/0 hooks and large squid and mackerel baits will bring better results.

SPOTTED RAY
There are five commonly caught rays in our waters ranging from a few pounds in weight to over 30 lbs. The smallest is the spotted ray that rarely grows over 5lbs. It is a light beige colour, covered in dark spots that don't extend to the edge of the wings.

Spotted ray are normally caught while fishing with a flowing trace for bream and other small fish. They will take squid, mackerel, crab or ragworm, and on light tackle can be fun to catch.

SMALL-EYED
The small-eyed ray, once known as the painted ray, is pale brown with a few light blotches and a double row of thin white lines near the edge of the wings. They grow to about 15 lbs and in summer come into inshore waters, where there is a mixture of sand and boulders, to breed. Small-eyed ray will feed on mackerel and squid but their favourite is sand eel. Fish with a dead or frozen sand eel on a metre long trace with a 2/0 or 3/0 hook, over a sand bank or where there's a mixture of sand and boulders. From June to September the small-eyed ray produces an egg sack, like the 'mermaid's purse', near weedy rocks or boulders where it attaches itself until it's time for the immature ray to emerge.

UNDULATE
The most dramatically marked ray in our seas is the undulate ray. Growing to near 20 lbs these rays have bold brown lines and marks on a pale grey-brown background. The undulate ray breeds from March to September. It's not easy to target undulate rays but in an area where they have been caught previously a mackerel or squid bait are the best options to try.

THORNBACK
Our most common and widely distributed ray is the thornback, or roker as it's known in many parts. Identified by a row of sharp thorns down its backbone and tail with several others on the wings.

Colouration can be confusing as many have light and dark spots and blotches all over while others may only have one or two. Thornback ray are found in fairly shallow water over clean ground and sandbanks, moving some way into estuaries. They take a wide range of baits depending where they are. In estuaries the best bait is a prawn while they will take any fish bait or crab out at sea. In the early part of the year rays in the Thames estuary, for example, are quite keen on a chunk of fresh herring. Other baits that will take thornbacks are a mix of ragworm and sand eel, peeler crab, squid, mackerel and even lugworm tipped with squid. Traces should be about a metre of 20 lb to 30 lb mono with a 2/0 hook.

BLONDE RAY
Our biggest ray is the blonde ray. They are caught on deep-water banks and prefer an area with strong tides. Colouration is a yellowish brown with small dark spots that go right to the edge of the wings. A blonde ray is a considerable adversary as they live in areas of strong tides and can run to over 30 lbs. By using their full wingspan to kite in the tide can be a very difficult job to get to the surface. The longer the fight goes on the more likely the trace will wear through and many good fish are lost if there's any weakness in the tackle. The best rig is a simple running leger with a trace of about a metre long and a 4/0 to 6/0 hook baited with a cocktail of mackerel and squid.

COMMON SKATE
The biggest fish we are likely to encounter in UK waters is the massive common skate that are

regularly caught weighing up to 200lbs. For such a large fish they are found in very localised areas and a long term tagging programme has shown that they don't venture far. This makes them easy to locate and means they need protecting and are always returned to the sea after capture. Anyone wanting to catch a big skate needs to travel to Scotland where Oban is the skate capital with several charter boats available and properly equipped. Proper tackle is needed to tackle the skate with 50 lb class rods, large capacity reels loaded with 50 lb braid and a 12/0 hook bait with a whole dogfish or pollack. Once a skate is hooked the battle really begins to get them off the bottom and a harness and butt pad are essential to get the fish moving and save the angler from harm.

CONGER EEL

One of the most feared and fantasised about fish in our waters is the mighty conger eel. They are found on rocky reefs, wartime wrecks and round deepwater piers where they lay in wait for their prey. While the tide is running they generally lay up but start to move out to forage during the slack tide period. Most big congers are caught from the boats but many fish over 50 lb have been landed from the shore, mostly at night from piers, under bridges and in marinas. Congers are a very powerful fish and need suitable tackle to take them on. Modern rods are so powerful and flexible that a 20lb to 30lb class rod will cope with all but the very biggest eels. The rod should be matched to a large lever drag reel such as a Shimano 15 or 20, loaded with 50 lb braid and five metres of 30 lb to 50 lb mono as a leader. The mono leader is far more abrasion resistant than braid so if it comes against any rocks or wreckage it may get scuffed but should remain strong enough to beat the eel. Conger eels are very fussy about what they eat and the fresher the bait the better. A mackerel cut into a flapper is the most widely used bait, but for the bigger fish try a large pouting, cuttlefish or scad. It's easy to forget how powerful a big conger can be so make sure a butt pad is on hand to strap on, as the butt of the rod can easily bruise the stomach or groin when levering against a large eel.

LING

One of the largest fish many anglers will ever catch is a ling. They grow to over 30lbs and are found round the numerous wrecks around our coastline where they will feed on any small fish they come across. The best way to catch one is drifting over a wreck with a luminous muppet or lure baited with a fillet of mackerel. The first sign of a ling is a tentative pluck on the line; if the rod is gently raised the fish will grab at the bait and hook itself as it tries to pull the bait down to the wreck. They can be caught using a paternoster rig with hooks on short traces above the weight or with a metre long flowing trace. They give a good account of themselves and require a strong trace to prevent them biting through it.

GURNARD

The three species of gurnard most likely to be caught in UK waters are the tub gurnard that are the largest, the red gurnard and the smaller grey gurnard. Others do turn up occasionally such as the streaked gurnard but generally the first three mentioned are the most common. Many gurnard are caught on baited feathers as they are an aggressive fish but to target them it's normal to use a flowing trace with a smallish hook and bait with a sliver of fresh mackerel. To identify the three types, the tub gurnard is a dull red with large pectoral fins edged with a distinct blue line. They also grow to double figures although a fish of 5lbs or more is exceptional. The red gurnard is also red but doesn't have such large pectoral fins and can be identified by a bright yellow colour inside the gill cover. The grey gurnard is usually caught in deeper water, is a much duller colour and has a very spiny lateral line. Despite their bony appearance, gurnard are in fact a very tasty fish to eat.

RED BANDFISH
One of the more unusual fish you could come across is the red bandfish. It has a fairly small head and very long tapered body that is dark red along the back and yellowish below. It feeds on small crustaceans and worms found while burrowing in muddy areas. These are usually caught by accident when fishing for small fish like bream with ragworm or small strips of squid.

JOHN DORY
This is another unusual looking fish, with elongated dorsal fin and a large spot on its side. Looked at from the front it has a very slim profile that it uses to creep up on other fish, then using its extraordinary extending mouth it engulfs its victim. John Dory can be caught using live baits, artificial lures such as shad or even a set of hokkais.

CONCLUSION

In this small book we have explained how to go about pier, shore and boat fishing. There are separate sections on the baits to use, the tackle required, the species of fish you may catch and what to do if you catch a potential record. Now it's down to you the angler to take a bit from each section, and get out there and put the knowledge gained to use. You will need to take the best points, add them to your own ideas, and with a little bit of luck and a degree of patience you can enjoy the thrill of catching fish on a regular basis. Fishing is a healthy sport that gets you out in the fresh air, giving you plenty of exercise as some fishing spots require a long walk, and eating part of your catch can add to a healthy diet. Tight lines.

JIM WHIPPY